Robert M. Reed

LINCOLN'S FUNERAL TRAIN

The Epic Journey from Washington to Springfield

Schiffer Publishing Ltd

4880 Lower Valley Road • Atglen, PA 19310

Contents page caption:

An illustration shows soldiers voting in the 1864 presidential election. President Lincoln received an overwhelming nearly 78 percent of the soldier vote that year among the ten states that allowed military voting. Soldier votes in Kansas and Minnesota arrived too late to be counted that year. Lincoln's body was later moved 17 times from his fatal wounding at Ford's Theatre to his tomb in Springfield—most of the time in the caring arms of soldiers. *Federal Bureau of National Literature and Art.*

Other Schiffer Books by the Author:
The United States Presidents Illustrated.
978-0-7643-3280-7 $29.99

Other Schiffer Books on Related Subjects:
The Paranormal Presidency of Abraham Lincoln.
Christopher Kiernan Coleman.
978-0-7643-4121-2 $16.99

Abraham Lincoln: An Illustrated Biography in Postcards.
James D. Ristine.
978-0-7643-2857-2 $24.95

Copyright © 2014 by Robert M. Reed

Library of Congress Control Number: 2014938200

Designed by John P. Cheek
Cover Design by RoS

Type set in News Goth Cn BT/Georgia

ISBN: 978-0-7643-4594-4
Printed in the United States of America

Published by Schiffer Publishing, Ltd.
4880 Lower Valley Road
Atglen, PA 19310
Phone: (610) 593-1777; Fax: (610) 593-2002
E-mail: Info@schifferbooks.com

For our complete selection of fine books on this and related subjects, please visit our website at www.schifferbooks.com. You may also write for a free catalog.

This book may be purchased from the publisher. Please try your bookstore first.

We are always looking for people to write books on new and related subjects. If you have an idea for a book, please contact us at proposals@schifferbooks.com

Schiffer Publishing's titles are available at special discounts for bulk purchases for sales promotions or premiums. Special editions, including personalized covers, corporate imprints, and excerpts can be created in large quantities for special needs. For more information, contact the publisher.

This dedication is a salute to both the past and present.

This book first is dedicated to the uncounted millions who braved the weather and often the darkness of night to pay their last respects to President Abraham Lincoln. These faceless mourners, whose exact numbers will never be known, give us pride yet today. They came by carriage, horseback, wagon, or just on foot for a glimpse of the Lincoln Funeral Train. They bowed their heads, said their prayers, and sang their songs of sorrow.

In addition, this book is dedicated to the groups, large and small, around the nation that continue to preserve and promote our precious American history from the community to the classroom. In that spirit, let me single out my own hometown's Historic Knightstown Incorporated. Those leaders who continue to rescue and maintain local history include Kathie Rummel, Bill Sitler, Joann Smith, David Steele, Barbara Carter, Robert Brown, Carol Renfro, and Peg Mayhill. Associate leaders are Bob Myers and Reid Brennan.

For your service, I thank you. It has been a privilege.

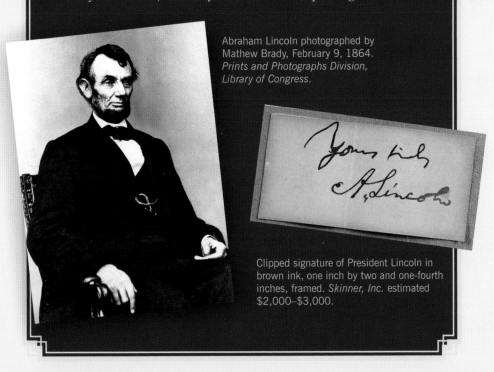

Abraham Lincoln photographed by Mathew Brady, February 9, 1864. *Prints and Photographs Division, Library of Congress.*

Clipped signature of President Lincoln in brown ink, one inch by two and one-fourth inches, framed. *Skinner, Inc.* estimated $2,000–$3,000.

"*Everywhere deep sorrow has been manifested, and the feeling seems, if possible, to deepen, as we move westward with the remains to their final resting place.*"

—*The New York Times*, April 28, 1865

A painted Union shield frame, depicting a lithograph portrait of Abraham Lincoln, from latter 19th century. Size, 24 by 18 inches. *Skinner, Inc*. estimated $400–$600.

Contents

Postcard of an original portrait of Abraham Lincoln, then depicted by George Henry Story. Original portrait located at the Henry E. Huntington Library and Art Gallery in San Marino, California.

A classic campaign banner of the 1860 presidential election that proclaims support for Old Abe, Prince of Rails. Lincoln was the first Republican candidate to be elected president. *Skinner, Inc.*

Foreword

The sesquicentennial of Abraham Lincoln's tenure as President and the Civil War years has renewed interest in the history of the era with a proliferation of books, articles, movies, and documentaries. Most narratives focus on the presidency or the battles of the Civil War. Robert M. Reed takes a different approach. His *Lincoln's Funeral Train* provides a poignant account of Lincoln's final journey. The book, like his seventeen others, affords first-hand accounts as well as vivid illustrations of the period using various forms of paper ephemera from early photo reproductions preserved by the Library of Congress to vintage magazine prints by *Harper's Weekly*.

The year 1865 was a simpler time. There were no TV news flashes, radio broadcasts, telephone calls, emails, instant-messaging, tweets, or twitters. The news of Lincoln's assassination and details of the funeral preparations were telegraphed around the country, printed in local newspapers, and finally passed by word-of-mouth. Thus, the population of the Midwest learned the detailed itinerary of the funeral train and grasped the opportunity to pay reverence to their beloved President. Robert Reed and I have lived in the shadow of the funeral train's path all of our lives. Stories have been carried down through generations of our ancestors to bestow insight about the importance of this event in the many states it touched.

Reed provides a perspective about the Lincoln Funeral Train that is more than just a description of the physical voyage, but rather one about the people who came to view the cortege. The impact of the assassination could not be further emphasized than by the respect hundreds of thousands of Americans conveyed by assembling for formal tributes in large cities or by gathering along a railroad crossing in the middle of a rainy, chilly, April night to gaze as the Lincoln Special slowly passed.

The anticipation of the train's arrival at rural junctions must have been overwhelming as the simple folk, both black and white, awaited the sound of the pilot train to signal the cortege's arrival. The image of hundreds standing silently at 3 a.m. hoping for a glimpse of the draped funeral car—even these many, many years later—is chilling. As the train neared, a soulful sound often emerged as many folk began to sing low and mournful hymns. One can almost whiff the overpowering scent of exotic flowers surrounding the casket, which at the end of the 13-day journey must have been mingled with the hint of the deteriorating remains in the period before modern embalming.

Reed captures images of the transit of the funeral train and the memorials at large cities through his depiction of events and the responses, moods, and feelings of the populace along the journey—not only declarations of the politicians and clergy delivering formal elegies, but also the thoughts and musings of the common folk who came to honor their fallen leader. For the mourners, the observance would be the most important event of their lives and one they would recollect in letters, stories, and vestiges, carried down through their family lines. *Lincoln's Funeral Train* provides the reader with accounts and personal stories appealing to everyone interested in these remarkable events.

—Dr. Elma Lee Schmidt Moore, PhD,
Dean Emeritus, Wittenberg University
August 19, 2013

An oval shaped print of Abraham Lincoln as he appeared in 1861. Image was issued by the long since defunct Federal Bureau of National Literature and Art.

Acknowledgments

Somewhere in this wonderful country tucked away in one family's heirlooms is a swath of black draping from the actual Lincoln Funeral Train. Legend has it that this bit of cloth was snipped by a great-great grandmother who had secreted a pair of scissors beneath her apron and cloak when the train pulled into her village's train depot.

The descendents of this woman shared this story with me during my years of researching the journey of the immortal Lincoln Funeral Train. They asked me not to use any names however, "Because maybe good old Grandma shouldn't have done it, but she probably wasn't the only one."

No doubt many, many other people along the way were likewise tempted to clip bits of the historic mourning cloth either from the train itself, or at other settings when the President's remains were viewed.

The "snipping" is just one of numerous stories shared with me involving families who were able to recall the accounts of ancestors who had actually encountered the funeral train. And in turn their stories were passed down over the generations.

Here is another example.

Award-winning journalist Donna Cronk, who has been long supportive of this book's preparation, has written of such a generational story in the *New Castle* (IN) *Courier Times*. Her grandmother had told her tales of the grandmother's own mother, Sally Ann. As the story went, Sally Ann got up in the middle of the night and went to see the Lincoln Funeral Train as it passed by in 1865. Since Sally Ann did not immediately live close to any railroad tracks, the family more or less dismissed the account until Donna Cronk discovered the actual train route was really only about ten miles away from where the young woman's home had been back in 1865. Given all the facts, it is now very plausible that Sally Ann made the trip, maybe by buggy or horse-drawn wagon, during that remarkable night and remembered for the rest of her life.

Someday there could still be a book on the remembrances of friends and family members who have verbal or written accounts of those who actually witnessed the Lincoln Funeral Train.

Others who have shared enlightening information include Richard P. Ratcliff of Spiceland, Indiana; Mrs. Malcom Jeffers of Richmond, Indiana; John Resh, logistics coordinator of the Wayne County Tourism Bureau, Richmond, Indiana; Carol McConahan Rhodes of Centerville, Indiana; Pat Chase of Sulphur Springs, Texas; Charles Sullivan of Raysville, Indiana; Ms. Leah Huddleston of Cambridge City, Indiana; and Mary Craven of Knightstown, Indiana—to name a few.

Special appreciation to Heather P. Reed, the mother of my wonderful grandchildren, who has contributed to the editorial function of Antique and Collectible News Service for many years, along with the editing of this book and many of my previous books.

My kindest thanks also, to Dr. Elma Lee Moore, dean emeritus of Wittenberg University. Dr. Moore, a most knowledgeable person, has befriended me for many years, and responded to my request by thoughtfully writing this book's foreword.

A note of appreciation also to Indiana State Representative Tom Saunders, a history buff himself.

Eternal thanks to Skinner, Inc., one of the nation's foremost auctioneers and appraisers of objects of value (www.skinnerinc.com, which has been generous with information and illustrations for our own Antique and Collectible News Service for more than 20 years. A note of appreciation also to Swann Auction Galleries, (www.swanngalleries.com), another fine firm and source of historic images for decades.

Recognition also to Early American History Store auctions at EarlyAmerican. com., Lincoln Highway National Museum & Archives (www.lincoln-highwaymuseum.org), Wikipedia encyclopedia, and Mike Leavy of Lima, New York, Genesse designs.

In researching this book, there has been heavy reliance on contemporaneous material published either during the actual time of the Lincoln Funeral Train's journey or shortly afterwards.

This would include numerous periodical accounts, particularly of newspapers in various communities who often deployed journalists to ride on the train itself or be present either directly at the depot or among the mourners themselves in various locations. Equally important were the books published immediately after the assassination and the following historic funeral rites. Among them were: *Lincoln Memorial: The Journeys of Abraham Lincoln From Springfield to Washington; and from Washington to Springfield*, 1865 by William Conggshall; *The Parricides: or, the Doom of the Assassins, the Authors of the Nation's Loss* by Ned Buntline, 1865; *The Lincoln Memorial, A Record of Life, Assassination, and Obsequies of the Martyred President*, 1865; *Memorial Record of the Nation's Tribute to Abraham Lincoln* by B. F. Morris, 1865; *Illustrated Life, Services, Martyrdom, and Funeral of Abraham Lincoln* published by T. B. Peterson, 1865; *Abraham Lincoln: His Life, Public Services, Death and Great Funeral Cortege* by John Power; *The Terrible Tragedy at Washington: Assassination of Abraham Lincoln*, 1865; *Obsequies of Abraham Lincoln, in the City of New York by David Valentine*, 1865; and *The Assassination of President Lincoln and the Trial of Conspirators* by Benn Pittman, 1865.

There were understandably a great number of other resources (see bibliography)

and a sea of other books and related material regarding President Abraham Lincoln who remains the most written about person in the unique history of the United States.

A special thanks and note of appreciation is extended to the Library of Congress and their treasury of historic Civil War and post-Civil War photographs so richly preserved and maintained.

Additionally, an ongoing gratitude for a great range of historical associations and organizations, starting with Historical Knightstown, Inc. and the Henry County Historical Society, along with numerous other county, regional, and state historical organizations that doggedly continue to preserve this country's great heritage.

A vintage postcard of Abraham Lincoln showing as he went ultimately from a log cabin to The White House. When Lincoln took office in March of 1861, five former presidents were still living: James Buchanan, Franklin Pierce, Millard Fillmore, John Tyler, and Martin Van Buren.

Introduction

Print of photograph taken of Lincoln in early April of 1865. *Library of Congress.*

As the story goes, the tiny village of Dublin, Indiana, turned out just about every one of its citizens when the black-draped Lincoln Funeral Train passed in virtually the dead of night in April 1865.

The citizens of Dublin were lined up shoulder-to-shoulder on both sides of the railroad track as the Lincoln Special rolled into town with its lone bell tolling. It was shortly after 4 a.m. and a cold rain had begun falling. As the hearse car bearing President Abraham Lincoln's body slowly pulled into view, some standing there prayed, some softly sang hymns, and most every person cried.

Just months earlier, in the presidential election of 1864, the people of Dublin were steadfast. They cast 269 votes for President Lincoln and zero votes for his opponent, General George McClellan. In the heartland of the country, they were as loyal to the President as anyone could possibly be.

Billhead of the National Drill Company located in 19th century Dublin, Indiana, for a shipment to Knightstown, Indiana. Both towns were on the Lincoln Funeral Train route.

Classic map of the Lincoln Funeral Train as presented in the 1872 edition of The Life of Lincoln and his *Great Funeral Cortege*. The book was written by John Carroll Power.

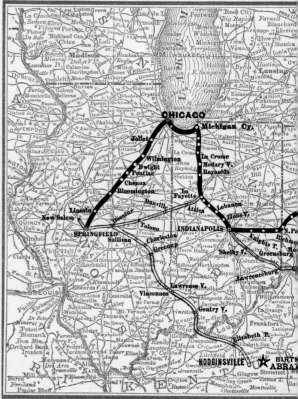

God bless President Lincoln, said the folks in Dublin.

It was like that with the Lincoln Funeral Train.

That fateful train, officially called The Lincoln Special, traveled eventually through more than 440 cities, towns, villages, and byways, bearing the body of President Lincoln back to his hometown of Springfield, Illinois.

The extraordinary Lincoln Train trip took 13 days and covered nearly 1,700 miles of America, from thriving cities to isolated crossroads. Millions came out to see the funeral train, far more than were expected in the initial planning. They not only stood in the streets and beside the train depots; they stood along the railways in vast open spaces of the countryside. They stood in the cold April rain. They stood in the middle of the night. They stood, as one eye-witness account declared, "not just there by the thousands, but there by the acres."

On the whole, the entire operation was remarkable.

The Lincoln Train departed the nation's capital one morning and traveled a near whale-shaped course through Maryland, Pennsylvania, New Jersey, New York, Ohio, Indiana, and finally Illinois There were large ceremonies, which drew hundreds of thousands of people in cities like Baltimore, Harrisburg, Philadelphia, New York, Albany, Buffalo, Cleveland, Columbus, Indianapolis, and Chicago. And there were small trackside ceremonies, which may have only included the occupants of a few farm wagons.

Through the intricate planning of the War Department, the Lincoln Funeral Train passed through the eastern half of the country largely on schedule, with crowds eagerly awaiting its arrival. On and on it went passing, at times, endless lines of mourners.

The train maintained its course the entire time defended by little more than a pilot train running just ahead of the Lincoln Special itself. There were no incidents, no angry mobs, no rock throwing, no blockades, and no jeers. Even after years of a bitter Civil War struggle that had divided a nation, communities, and even families—there were no major disruptions of that train's mission.

This book is about that remarkable journey.

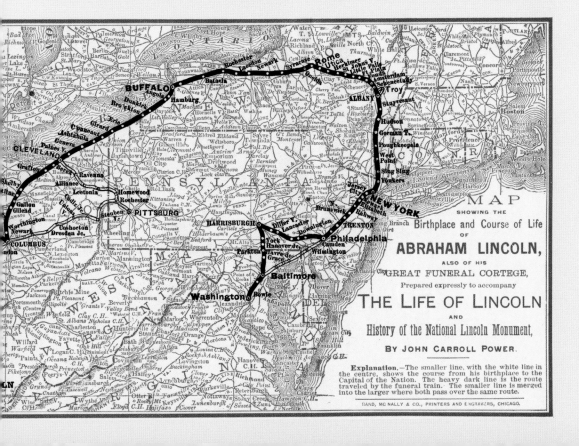

Journey Begins
(Washington, D.C.)

*April is the cruelest month, breeding
Lilacs out of the dead land, mixing
Memory and desire, stirring
Dull roots with spring rain.*

—T.S. Eliot

April of 1865 was a cruel month.

It would begin with a horrible war still continuing, still churning up souls and spitting out lives. It harmed all that it touched, and it touched everyone—even the children.

During the Civil War more than two million soldiers were age 21 and younger according to military historians. More than one million of those were 18 or younger, and an estimated more than 800,000 were between the ages of 17 and 16 or even younger. Standards were low and record-keeping was laxer still.

It was likewise with the dead.

Certainly the Civil War, which at last reached its final stages in April, had taken more American lives than any conflict before it (or after it through the 20th century). For years, historians recorded the death total at more than 600,000 lives. Nobody could be sure. There was no accurate count within the limited means of the mid-19th century military or governing bodies.

Watercolor on paper, signed A. Lincoln and inscribed "Sketched Sept. 23 1864." The sketch, 11 by 9 inches, is signed by at the lower right by H. Balling. Attached to the sketch was a 1871 letter from Balling designating the art work for the New York Artists' Chicago Relief Fund. Balling is best known for his portraiture work, *Heroes of the Republic,* which depicted General U.S. Grant and other generals, now in the Smithsonian Institution at Washington. *Skinner, Inc.,* estimated $15,000–$20,000.

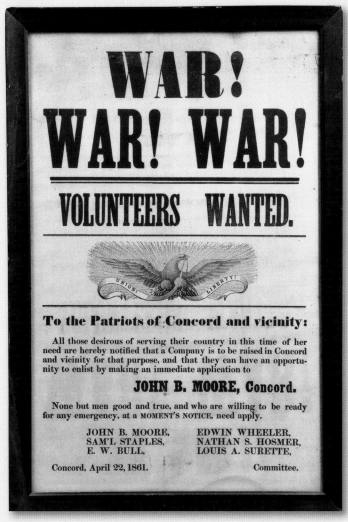

Civil War recruiting broadside, framed, from Massachusetts, April 22, 1861. Inscribed Union Liberty and featuring an eagle. About 12 by 19 inches in size. *Skinner, Inc.*

In more recent years, estimates of the Civil War dead, including soldiers as well as civilians, have been higher. One scholar, J. David Hacker, a professor of history at Binghamton University in New York, has written that the ultimate death count, if done accurately at the time, could have been anywhere from 650,000 to 850,000.

Whatever the exact number, by April of 1865 it affected nearly every family in America.

Besides the deceased, there were the fathers, sons, and brothers who somehow survived but were however crippled by the ravages of the Civil War. Even by April there were few or no able-bodied men living in some counties of the country. The male population in some of those areas consisted of those under 16, those few elderly who had been too old for war, and those physically disabled former soldiers who had been disabled through loss of limbs, similar war-related injury, or disease.

That was not even counting war injuries of the mind—just as disabling and fearsome—which were not even truly recognized in the 1860s medical world.

The long war and its accompanying tragedies appeared to be waning on April 9, when Confederate General Robert E. Lee surrendered to Union General U.S. Grant. Back in Washington, where President Abraham Lincoln's earlier inaugural speech had stirringly stressed "with malice toward none, with charity for all," there was some feeling of relief after long suffering.

In the days immediately following the early April surrender President Lincoln had visited the fallen Confederate center in Richmond, Virginia. He returned somewhat buoyed about the future.

The month of April 1865 found President Lincoln both loved and hated. But at least he had the divided country's full attention.

Back in the presidential election of 1860 Lincoln was elected with less than 40 percent of the vote. He was one of four candidates on the ballot in the Northern states and not even on the ballot in what would eventually be Confederate states. In order to build on his identity and hopefully popularity it was planned that his 1861 inaugural train-trip to Washington be a free-wheeling tour that would touch as many populous locations as possible.

On the way to the White House that year, the president-elect rode the train across the countryside with stops in places like Indianapolis, Cleveland, Philadelphia, Buffalo, and New York City. Generally, the pre-inaugural trip was successful. Crowds cheered and cannons boomed.

However despite the overall enthusiasm along the way, there were dissenters. During much of the last 200 miles of the journey, Lincoln was embarrassingly forced to wear a disguise to avoid perceived threats in Baltimore.

Throughout his days in the White House the threats against President Lincoln never ceased.

In December of 1864, at that point just months earlier than the actual assassination, this notice had chillingly ran in the *Selma (Alabama) Dispatch*:

"One Million Dollars Wanted. To Have Peace by the First of March.

"If the citizens of the Confederacy will furnish me with the cash, or good securities of the sum of one million dollars. I will cause the lives of Abraham Lincoln, William H. Seward and Andrew Johnson to be taken by the First of March next.

"This will give us peace, and satisfy the world that cruel tyrants cannot live in a land of liberty. If this is not accomplished, nothing will be claimed beyond the sum of fifty thousand dollars in advance, which is supposed to be necessary to reach and slaughter the three villains.

"I will give myself one thousand dollars towards this patriotic purpose. Everyone wishing to contribute will address Box X, Conaba, Alabama."

And then a little more than a month before Lee's surrender in Virginia this news item ran in the *Philadelphia North American*. It was dated March 8, 1865.

"Washington–

"A man named Clements has been turned over to the civil authorities by the military, against whom the evidence is positive that he had all his plans arranged for the assassination of the President on Inauguration Day. He is in jail here.

"Clements and another person came from Alexandria, Virginia on Saturday. They were both extremely disorderly, and seemed to have been drinking freely. Clements in particular, was very abusive, and said, using gross and profane language, that he came here to assassinate the President, that he was late by one-half hour, and that his Savior would never forgive him for failing to do so; that he would do it that night, namely the fifth of March, and that he came expressly to do it, and he would do it before he left town."

Nevertheless, life continued at the White House for President Lincoln, both officially and socially.

On the morning of Friday, April 14, the *National Daily Intelligence* newspaper reported to their Washington area readers that Miss Laura Keene would be making her last appearance in the current play *Our American Cousin* at the Ford Theatre.

ASSASSINATION OF PRESIDENT LINCOLN APRIL 14, 1865.

FORD'S THEATRE DRAPED IN MOURNING

Vintage postcard of the assassination of President Lincoln, April 14, 1865. Also depicted is Ford's Theatre draped in mourning. Reverse bears a narrative of the assassination. $25–$50.

That same evening the *Washington Evening Star* reported this brief news item:

"Lieutenant General Grant, President and Mrs. Lincoln have secured the state box at Ford's Theatre tonight, to witness Miss Laura Keene's American Cousin."

There is some speculation that assassin John Wilkes Booth may have read the notice while a patron at the National Hotel in Washington. At any rate it is likely that Booth learned of the President's attendance from other sources. And, of course, the news report was only partially correct: General Grant instead had left Washington with Mrs. Grant and did not attend the event at Ford's Theatre.

President Lincoln and his wife, Mary Todd Lincoln, did however attend. It would

be a cruel ending to a night in April. The fatal shot that would ultimately take the life of President Lincoln was fired sometime after 10 p.m. As the 16th president of the United States, he was the first to have ever been shot down by an assassin's bullet.

Minutes after the President was shot at the theatre, a series of telegrams began going out to newspapers across the country. A major source of these telegrams was the *Associated Press* which mutually served membership newspapers.

Initially known as *New York Associated Press*, the service cooperative shared news-gathering expenses with various daily newspapers. They were operating a branch in Washington not far from Ford's Theatre.

On that fearful Friday night, *Associated Press* correspondent Lawrence A. Gobright was on duty at the AP office. His dispatches were at first based on those people who rushed into the office. After the first dispatch, or "special," he ran to the theatre and later filed other reports.

The *New-York Tribune* carried the over-night dispatches on the following morning:

FIRST DISPATCH
HIGHLY IMPORTANT!
The President Shot!
Secretary Seward Attacked.
Washington, April 14, 1865

SECOND DISPATCH
The President was shot in a theatre tonight and perhaps mortally wounded.
To Editors: Our Washington Agent orders the dispatch about the President "stopped." Nothing is said about the truth of the report.

THIRD DISPATCH
Special to the *New-York Tribune*:
The President was just shot at Ford's Theatre. The ball entered his neck. It is not known whether the wound is mortal. Intense excitement.

FOURTH DISPATCH
Special to the *New-York Tribune*:
The President expired at a quarter to twelve.

FIFTH DISPATCH
To the *Associated Press*:
The President was shot in a theatre tonight and perhaps mortally wounded.

The President is not expected to live through the night.

He was shot at a theatre.

Secretary Seward was also assassinated.

No arteries were cut.

Particulars soon.

Washington, April 15, 12:30 a.m.

SIXTH DISPATCH
Special to the *New-York Tribune*
Washington, Friday, April 14, 1865

"Like a clap of thunder out of a clear sky spread the announcement that President Lincoln was shot while sitting in a box at Ford's Theatre. The city is wild with excitement. A gentleman who was present thus describes the event: 'At about ten and a half o'clock, in the midst of one of the acts, a pistol shot was heard, and at the same instant a man leaped upon the stage from the same box occupied by the President, brandished a long knife, and shouted, "Sic simper tyrannis!," then rushed to the rear of the scenes and out of the back door to the theatre.'

So sudden was the whole thing that most persons in the theatre supposed it a part of the play, and it was some minutes before the fearful tragedy was comprehended. The man was pursued, however, by someone connected with the theatre to the outer door and seemed to mount a horse and ride rapidly away. A regiment of cavalry have started in all directions, with orders to arrest every man found on horse-back."

Some of the dispatches were correct, while others, filed in the uproarious minutes after the presidential assassination, were woefully incorrect. President Lincoln clearly did not die in the theatre. He died the following Saturday morning as he lay across a bed in a boarding house across the street from Ford's Theatre. The time was shortly after 7 a.m.

Ford's Theatre in April of 1865, draped with crepe following the assassination of President Lincoln at that building in Washington, D.C. *Library of Congress photograph.*

The shooting of President Abraham Lincoln occurred four years to the day of the surrender of Fort Sumter, which had then marked the beginning of the long and brutal Civil War.

About one hour after being officially pronounced dead, the body of President Lincoln was removed from the boarding house and taken to the White House. There the body underwent autopsy and preparation for eventual public viewing. Actually the body would be moved numerous times before arriving at its final resting place in Springfield, Illinois.

Meanwhile, the country was reacting to the horrible event. The week in the North had begun with celebrations of the winding down of the war. In Philadelphia, for example, there were reports of "rejoicing bordering frenzy... hosannas of praise in behalf of our victorious armies ...and excitement over the approaching illumination to commemorate the nation's deliverance..."

Then came the news of the shooting of President Lincoln. The *Philadelphia Public Ledger* later recalled it this way: "The sad story was known to but a few persons Friday night. Outside of the newspaper offices it did not spread very far, but with the break of day (Saturday) the newsboys' cry awoke the people to a knowledge of the tragedy. It was with difficulty that men could be made to believe the story. That such an event could occur at the capital of the nation was hard to comprehend, and men and women took counsel together at early dawn, and with tearful eyes and saddened countenances prayed that there might be some mistake.

"Soon people found their way to the heart of the city to learn the full extent of the tragedy. Work was suspended in workshop and factory; county houses and brokers' offices were closed;

merchants closed their stores, and everybody crowded to the newspaper offices, to catch the first announcement of a possible improvement in the President's condition.

"Past political differences were forgotten in the universal sorrow, and men discussed the event as a national humiliation and shame. Sadness was visible on every face. When the *Official Gazette* put to rest all hopes by announcing the death of Mr. Lincoln, the grief of the people was manifest in all directions.

"Strong and brave men wept as they read the news, and the gleam of rage was seen to sparkle in the eyes of the more excitable. Within an hour after the announcement of Mr. Lincoln's death, Chestnut Street was draped in mourning.

"Heavy masses of black were suspended from every building. The newspaper offices set the example on the upper part of Chestnut Street, the white marble buildings, hung in black, presented a neat appearance.

"The crowd remained upon the street until after nightfall. The great anxiety appeared to be to learn whether the assassin had been captured.

Wanted poster broadside issued April 20, 1865 in Washington, D.C. It offers $100,000 reward for the "murderer of our late beloved President Abraham Lincoln." Some separations and losses, approximately 23 inches by 12 and a half inches. *Skinner, Inc.*

"Many of the city churches were heavily draped in mourning, though the black, in most of them, was tastefully arranged..."

Back in Washington elaborate funeral arrangements were being made and terse orders and proclamations were being issued. As suggested in Philadelphia, one of the first concerns nationally was to head off peace sounding celebrations and turn them to mourning. Earlier the governors of several Union states and the mayors of some cities had acted to issue proclamations declaring days of Thanksgiving upon the surrender of Confederate troops under the command of General Lee. Now it all had to be somehow countermanded.

One such "counter" measure came from the acting Secretary of State William Hunter in Washington. Hunter was acting on behalf of the seriously wounded (but not fatally wounded) Secretary Seward.

On Monday morning, April 17, Hunter had this message telegraphed around the country: "The undersigned is directed to announce that the funeral ceremonies of the lamented Chief Magistrate will take place at the Executive Mansion, in this city, at 12 o'clock noon, Wednesday, the nineteenth last. The various religious denominations throughout the country are invited to meet in their respective places of worship at the time, for purpose of solemnizing the occasion by appropriate ceremonies."

Wisely, the acting Secretary of State had commissioned all places of worship across the country to participate in what was to happen in the city of Washington, D.C.

Elsewhere in the White House, the coffin bearing the body of President Lincoln had been placed on a grand catafalque in the East Room. At 11 a.m. that Monday morning Chief Justice Salmon P. Chase administered the oath of office to President Andrew Johnson. Chase, a former Ohio governor and U.S. Senator, had served as Lincoln's Treasury Secretary the previous year before being nominated to the Supreme Court in December of 1864. An anxious and determined military

stepped in to regulate and detail the massive funeral service, which loomed the following Wednesday.

The assistant adjutant general of the War Department, W.A. Nichols, issued the following: "At sunrise on Wednesday, the nineteenth...a federal salute will be fired from the Military Stations in the vicinity of Washington, minute guns between the hours of 12 and 3 o'clock, and a national salute at the setting of the sun.

"The usual badge of mourning will be worn on the left arm, and on the hilt of the sword..."

Accordingly the War Department general established what would be the official procession on Wednesday following ceremonies in the White House. The first order of the procession would include one regiment of Cavalry, two batteries of Artillery, a battalion of Marines, and two regiments of Infantry.

Later on would come "dismounted officers" of various military agencies. Pallbearers would include members of the Senate and members of the House on either side of the Lincoln hearse. Immediately behind the hearse would be General U. S. Grant representing the Army and Admiral D.G. Farragut representing the Navy. Others of similar rank from both branches would follow.

Next would come civilians. This grouping would include family and relatives and delegations from the states of Illinois and Kentucky as mourners. Immediately following would be President Andrew Johnson, the cabinet, the diplomatic corps, and former presidents of the United States.

General Nichols' orders were explicit: "The troops designed to form the escort will assemble in the Avenue north of the President's house, and form (the) line precisely at 11 o'clock a.m. on Wednesday, the nineteenth, with the left resting on Fifteenth Street.

"The procession will move precisely at 2 o'clock p.m. on the conclusion of the religious services at the Executive Mansion appointed to commence at 12 o'clock meridian-when minute guns will be fired by detachments of artillery, stationed at St. John's Church, the City Hall, and at the Capitol. At the same hour, the bells of the several churches in Washington, Georgetown and Alexandria will be tolled."

The sun rose in Washington on the morning of Wednesday, April 19, but ultimately it would be rainy.

Stores were closed everywhere in the city that day as they had been since the assassination. Every public building was draped in black, and just about every residence was equally dressed in "somber crepe."

Thousands of people were teeming along the city's main streets, but for the most part they were subdued. As one observer later noted, "Sadness was depicted on every countenance, and soon the streets were thronged with military, societies, and citizens, winding their way to Pennsylvania Avenue and the White House."

Those actually invited to the funeral were required to have admission cards as the East Room assembly allowed only about 600 to be present. Those with the cards began assembling at about 10 a.m. The streets themselves were already crowded with military units preparing to form various sections of the funeral procession. The grand multitude of spectators were described as jammed together on sidewalks, but orderly.

It must have been fascinating to actually have been inside the East Room of the White House as the visitors filed to see for the first time the body of the slain President. This account given by an eye-witness was published later that year:

"The echoes of the funeral dirges in the distance seemed like the terrible murmur of the avenging God's wrath at the impiety of the awful crime that brought all here as mourners.

General U.S. Grant, who attended funeral services for President Lincoln in the White House. *Library of Congress photograph.*

"As the various delegations came in they quietly took the places assigned them. Not a word was spoken loudly. Whispers faint, as though the loved one was sleeping after his weary troubles and all feared to wake him, were the only noises that marred the death-like stillness of the room."

Certainly Lincoln was not the first American president to lie in state there in the East Room of the White House. William Henry Harrison and Zachary Taylor had both been there before him, and they had been formally and officially mourned. But Lincoln had been brutally murdered as a nation already mourned the great losses of the Civil War.

Correspondents who were admitted to the funeral scene in limited numbers would later describe seeing the president's son,

Line art illustration of Mrs. Mary Todd Lincoln. *Federal Bureau of National Literature and Art.*

Townsend. He had covered the Civil War for various newspapers and was filing dispatches for the *New York Herald* at the time of the Lincoln funeral.

The condition of the body was not just a matter of morbid curiosity. It was a matter of hard reality. The body would be above the ground for 20 days—something rarely if ever attempted by those who were practicing mortuary science during the middle of the 19th century. Eventually it would require the services of two full-time attendants working nearly around the clock to preserve the body in a state for viewing by millions of people.

As Townsend approached the casket of Lincoln, this is what he saw:

"Death has fastened into his frozen face all the character and idiosyncrasy of life. He has not changed one line of his grave, grotesque countenance, nor smoothed out a single feature.

"The hue is rather bloodless and leaden; but he was always sallow. The dark eyebrows seem abruptly arched; the beard, which will grow no more, is shaved close, save the tuft at the small short chin. The mouth is shut, like that of one who had put the foot down, and so are the eyes, which look as calm as slumber.

"The collar is short and awkward, turned over the stiff elastic cravat, and whatever energy or humor or tender gravity marked the living face is hardened into is pulse less outline. No corpse in the world is better prepared according to appearances. The white satin around it reflects sufficient light upon the face to show us that death is really there: but there are sweet roses and

Captain Robert Lincoln, weeping quietly with his face in his handkerchief. They also noted the absence of Lincoln's wife, Mary Todd Lincoln. In one account, she was recalled as "weak, worn, and nervous" and unable to gather herself enough to attend.

"She was the chief magistrate's lady yesterday," noted one observer, "today a widow bearing only an immortal name."

The center of attention that day in the East Room of the White House was of course the lifeless body of President Abraham Lincoln.

One of the most vivid descriptions came from veteran journalist George Alfred

Ticket or pass to the viewing of President Lincoln in the White House on April 19, 1865. *Skinner, Inc.* estimated $300–$500.

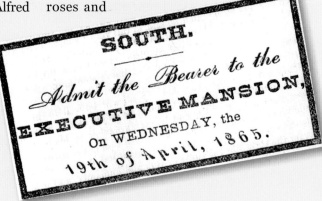

SOUTH.

Admit the Bearer to the EXECUTIVE MANSION, On WEDNESDAY, the 19th of April, 1865.

early magnolias, and the balmiest of lilies strewn around, as if the flowers had begun to bloom even upon his coffin."

Yet another reporter at the viewing noted that the President's features "retained their sweet, placid, natural expression, and the discoloration caused by the wound was slight as not to amount to disfigurement."

Inside, despite the admittance card requirement, there was a fairly diverse crowd of men and women, black and white, affluent and not-so-affluent, those who were high ranking in some level of government and those who might be considered in blunt terms to be simply rank.

Outside an even greater and more diverse mass of people struggled to find a view along the streets. They clung against posts, they filled narrow benches, and sat slumped on makeshift stools or wooden boxes. Beyond the street level they clambered on to roofs of smaller buildings, or bunched around upstairs windows for a sight of the long and somber procession.

Following services in the White House, and pretty much on schedule at 2 p.m., the procession began to move in order on Pennsylvania Avenue. With bells tolling in the distance, the parade of mourning took a full hour to pass the White House itself.

All proceeded solemnly. The hearse bearing the body of Lincoln was driven by six white horses. Aboard the hearse the coffin itself was elevated high enough to be seen by the masses that thronged both sides of the street. The floor of the hearse was covered with a swirl of white flowers and evergreens.

"Not less than five thousand officers, of every rank, marched abreast with the cortege," wrote correspondent Townsend of the sweeping Lincoln funeral procession in Washington.

"Never again, until Washington becomes in fact what it is in name, the chief city of America," continued Townsend, "shall we have a scene like this repeated—the grandest procession ever seen on this continent, spontaneously evoked to celebrate the foulest crime on record."

Crowds of mourners line the streets in Washington, D.C. for the funeral procession of President Abraham Lincoln in April of 1865. *Library of Congress photograph.*

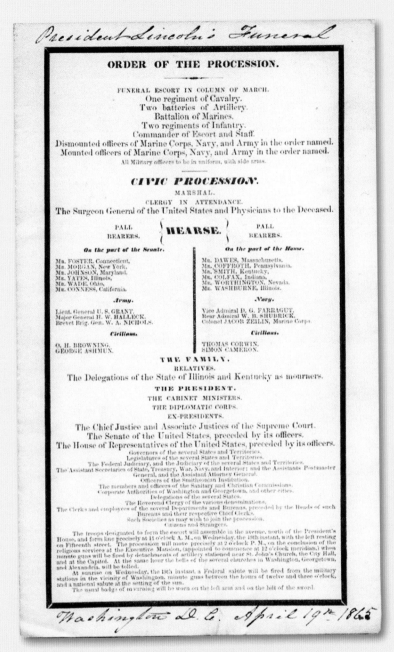

President Lincoln's Funeral

ORDER OF THE PROCESSION.

FUNERAL ESCORT IN COLUMN OF MARCH.
One regiment of Cavalry.
Two batteries of Artillery.
Battalion of Marines.
Two regiments of Infantry.
Commander of Escort and Staff.
Dismounted officers of Marine Corps, Navy, and Army in the order named.
Mounted officers of Marine Corps, Navy, and Army in the order named.
All Military officers to be in uniform, with side arms.

CIVIC PROCESSION.

MARSHAL.
CLERGY IN ATTENDANCE.
The Surgeon General of the United States and Physicians to the Deceased.

| PALL BEARERS. | { HEARSE. } | PALL BEARERS. |

On the part of the Senate.

Mr. FOSTER, Connecticut,
Mr. MORGAN, New York,
Mr. JOHNSON, Maryland,
Mr. YATES, Illinois,
Mr. WADE, Ohio,
Mr. CONNESS, California.

On the part of the House.

Mr. DAWES, Massachusetts,
Mr. COFFROTH, Pennsylvania,
Mr. SMITH, Kentucky,
Mr. COLFAX, Indiana,
Mr. WORTHINGTON, Nevada,
Mr. WASHBURNE, Illinois.

Army.

Lieut. General U. S. GRANT.
Major General H. W. HALLECK.
Brevet Brig. Gen. W. A. NICHOLS.

Navy.

Vice Admiral D. G. FARRAGUT.
Rear Admiral W. B. SHUBRICK.
Colonel JACOB ZEILIN, Marine Corps.

Civilians.

O. H. BROWNING.
GEORGE ASHMUN.

Civilians.

THOMAS CORWIN.
SIMON CAMERON.

THE FAMILY.

RELATIVES.
The Delegations of the State of Illinois and Kentucky as mourners.

THE PRESIDENT.
THE CABINET MINISTERS.
THE DIPLOMATIC CORPS.
EX-PRESIDENTS.
The Chief Justice and Associate Justices of the Supreme Court.
The Senate of the United States, preceded by its officers.
The House of Representatives of the United States, preceded by its officers.
Governors of the several States and Territories.
Legislatures of the several States and Territories.
The Federal Judiciary, and the Judiciary of the several States and Territories.
The Assistant Secretaries of State, Treasury, War, Navy, and Interior; and the Assistants Postmaster General, and the Assistant Attorney General.
Officers of the Smithsonian Institution.
The members and officers of the Sanitary and Christian Commissions.
Corporate Authorities of Washington and Georgetown, and other cities.
Delegations of the several States.
The Reverend Clergy of the various denominations.
The Clerks and employees of the several Departments and Bureaus, preceded by the Heads of such Bureaus and their respective Chief Clerks.
Such Societies as may wish to join the procession.
Citizens and Strangers.

The troops designated to form the escort will assemble in the avenue, north of the President's House, and form line precisely at 11 o'clock A. M., on Wednesday, the 19th instant, with the left resting on Fifteenth street. The procession will move precisely at 2 o'clock P. M., on the conclusion of the religious services at the Executive Mansion, (appointed to commence at 12 o'clock meridian,) when minute guns will be fired by detachments of artillery stationed near St. John's Church, the City Hall, and at the Capitol. At the same hour the bells of the several churches in Washington, Georgetown, and Alexandria, will be tolled.
At sunrise on Wednesday, the 19th instant, a Federal salute will be fired from the military stations in the vicinity of Washington, minute guns between the hours of twelve and three o'clock, and a national salute at the setting of the sun.
The usual badge of mourning will be worn on the left arm and on the hilt of the sword.

Washington D. C. April 19th 1865

Order of Procession for the President Lincoln funeral in Washington, D.C. Pallbearers were to walk alongside of the hearse. *Library of Congress.*

Townsend's eye-witness account further described the cortege as it passed the left side of the Capitol building, where it entered "the great gate, passed the grand stairway, opposite the splendid dome, where the coffin was disengaged and carried up the ascent."

Finally, it was slowly moved to the rotunda of the Capitol building and placed on a rather magnificent catafalque. It was an imposing sight for a crowd that stretched in all directions.

"This is a wonderful spectacle," added the Townsend dispatch.

Funeral procession of President Lincoln as it moves down Pennsylvania Avenue in April of 1865. *Library of Congress photograph.*

Crowd gathered at the U.S. Capitol building to view the funeral procession of President Lincoln in April of 1865. *Library of Congress photograph.*

Meanwhile, in cities and towns everywhere, variations of Lincoln's funeral services were underway nearly the same time as the President's remains reached the Capitol building.

Lincoln's hometown and the place that would be the final destination of the Funeral Train mirrored Washington. Local stores in Springfield were sold out of all available draping that could be used for buildings and houses. On the Statehouse, Governor's Mansion, Post Office, Arsenal, the military headquarters of General John Cook, and nearly all other structures in the town were "insignias of sorrow profusely displayed."

One account said the community of Springfield that day contained a "stillness, more profound than that of the Sabbath, and it reigned throughout the city."

After midday funeral services at numerous churches in Springfield, the city council met and passed an ordinance appropriating $20,000 to be expended to defray the expenses connected with the pending rites when the body of President Lincoln finally arrived there. In addition, artists were put to work decorating the Statehouse, both inside and out, "with proper mourning drapery."

Elsewhere in Springfield a group of citizens formed a committee to further expedite arrangements in connection with the then pending interment of President Lincoln's body. The committee was to further proceed with construction of a temporary vault "to be ready by the time the Funeral Train should arrive."

The committee officially called itself the National Lincoln Monument Association. Two days later they would issue a national appeal "by one simultaneous movement, testify its regard for his exalted character; its appreciation for his distinguished services, and its sorrow for his death, by erecting to his memory a monument that will forever prove that republics are not ungrateful."

Immediately, according to one account, "men labored upon the monument night and day, in order to have it ready by the time the funeral cortege was expected to arrive."

By contrast, there was no public mourning of President Lincoln in the Confederate seat of Richmond, Virginia.

According to the *Richmond* (Va.) *Whig*, there would be no such demonstration "because it is the desire of the military authorities that there shall be no assembly of the people of the city for the present." The city was then of course occupied by Union military forces.

The Whig added, however, that it had "heard expressions of grief on all sides, condemning and deploring the awful deed in unmeasured terms." It added that Lincoln's Assassination was "the heaviest blot which has ever fallen upon the people of the South."

Elsewhere, the *Philadelphia* (Pa.) *Public Ledger* commented: "It is hoped that our politicians will be sufficiently restrained by the National grief to defer their visits to President Johnson. The most of them seem to be impressed with the belief that their advice is absolutely necessary to enable him to administer the Government."

And while all these things are going on, the precise and intricate planning for the elaborate Lincoln Funeral Train was underway in the highest circles of the Federal Military.

On midnight of the day the Lincoln funeral ended in the East Room of the White House a message was telegraphed from Secretary of War Edwin Stanton to Major General John Adams Dix and others in authority.

The directive from who was then the most powerful figure in Washington made official mention and intention of the Lincoln Funeral Train. It read in part: "It has been finally concluded to conform to the original arrangements made yesterday (Tuesday) for the conveyance of the remains of President Abraham Lincoln from Washington to

Secretary of War Edwin Stanton in the 1860s. *Library of Congress photograph.*

Springfield by way of Baltimore, Harrisburg, Philadelphia, New York, Albany, Buffalo, Cleveland, Columbus, Indianapolis, Chicago to Springfield."

The terse message did not include all the hundreds of other little cities, towns, and byways that would make the trip even more historic and more real to the millions of citizens who would actually see the train and the actual Lincoln hearse car.

It did not start out to be a hearse car.

During the early months of 1865, a detachment of workers began a project for the United States military in nearby Alexandria, Virginia. The early construction plan was for a special train viewing car for Lincoln that could provide transportation for the president in various parts of the country.

Lincoln Funeral car especially prepared for the train journey departing Washington, D.C. *Library of Congress photograph.*

Certainly it was no ordinary car. It contained a parlor, a sitting room, and a sleeping apartment, "all of which was filled up in the most approved modern style," according to one report. Even the wheels of the car were especially made to fit on the various gauge (width) railroad tracks. Moreover, there were 16 wheels on the car, twice the number of traditional cars. This was an extremely helpful modification at the time since railroad track gauges varied from location to location.

There was a second car, of which there was relatively little written. It technically belonged to the Philadelphia, Wilmington & Baltimore railroad company, but was at the full disposal of the White House. It was intended for Lincoln

WILLIE LINCOLN, THIRD SON OF PRESIDENT LINCOLN.
DIED FEBRUARY 20, 1862, AT THE AGE OF 12.
From a photograph taken by Brady at Washington, shortly
before the death of Willie Lincoln.

Image of Willie Lincoln, whose body accompanied that of President Lincoln on the Lincoln Funeral Train. Matthew Brady photograph of Willie at age 12. *Library of Congress photograph.*

even the family car was "fitted up in the most elegant and costly manner."

Despite all the elaborate planning and construction, President Lincoln never even saw the car much less enjoyed the comforts of its transportation. One unconfirmed account suggests President Lincoln was to view and inspect the special car on the Saturday following his Friday evening visit to Ford's Theatre.

The assassination also immediately warranted dramatic changes in the decor of the train car. It was no longer the Presidential Car. It was now officially the Presidential Hearse Car.

The hearse car would be redone and it's numerous windows on both sides and at each end of the car would now be draped with black curtains. The entire furnishings of the hearse car inside would be shrouded in black for the entire trip.

As a matter of course, the car bearing Lincoln's body would always be the last car of the train before the caboose. Ahead of the hearse car would be baggage cars and various passengers. The order never changed and the passenger capacity remained at around 300 people, however additional cars could sometimes be added as the need arose.

Lincoln's body would not be the only corpse to make the trip on the Funeral Train.

Oddly, the hearse car would also include the body of William Wallace Lincoln. The child, affectionately known as Willie, died of typhoid fever during President Lincoln's second year in office. He was twelve years old at the time of his death, and his passing was a devastating event for Mr. and Mrs. Lincoln.

family or a Congressional committee. Before being refurbished for Federal use, it was available to the president of the railroad and the board directors of the rail company.

This "family" car contained four compartments, including a parlor, chamber, dining room, and kitchen. It was even equipped with water tanks. According to an observer,

Initially Mary Todd Lincoln had been severely opposed to the entire idea of a Lincoln Funeral Train, no matter how elaborately planned. She would not be consoled on the matter and only relented when those in charge agreed, at her frantic instance, to disinterment of the boy's body from a plot in Washington. The boy's body was placed in a different casket, which in turn would be placed alongside Lincoln's in the hearse car.

Mary Todd Lincoln, wife of President Lincoln, in Matthew Brady photograph from 1861. *Library of Congress photograph.*

Even at that Mrs. Lincoln refused to set foot on the Lincoln Funeral Train. The only immediate living family member to actually ride the train was son Robert. Ironically Robert would be the only family member not to be buried in the family plot at Springfield. Robert, with a distinguished public service record of his own, would ultimately be buried at Arlington National Cemetery.

The major figure of command regarding the Lincoln Funeral Train was the Lincoln Cabinet in general and Secretary of War Stanton in particular. The organization and structure behind the train's operation was the United States Military.

Stanton wanted the public to see President Lincoln.

In a way that was the whole point of the Lincoln Funeral Train: to let a mourning nation see President Lincoln, and to actually see his face as often as possible. It would be a part of the healing process not only for a nation that had lost a leader but also for a nation that had lost a part of its humanity in a long internal war.

Stanton and the military faced a vast amount of both personal and practical problems in attempting the across-the-nation train trip with the body of President Lincoln. Not to be indelicate, but one immediate problem was the steady and relentless decomposition of the body. It had been a concern even before the train trip.

As it turns out it would take two people on the train, embalmer Dr. Charles R. Brown and undertaker Frank T. Sands, working practically around the clock at every opportunity—when the train was moving or at least when the scene was closed off to the public—to keep the body viewable.

History records that millions of people at least viewed the passing Lincoln Funeral Train, and many of them were actually able to review the remains in the open casket. The exact number will never been known. The problem envisioned even before the train left the Washington station as the days (and nights) drug on and the crowds grew to the point that the casket was open longer and longer, it would leave attendants less and less time to upkeep the body. Understand too that the science of modern embalming was still in its very early stages.

One crude solution would be the near-constant addition of fresh flowers from the location at most every stop. Moreover, it also served a dual purpose of bathing the hearse car in a continuously pleasant scent.

Fresh flowers aside, here is still another early observation of the Lincoln body as it lay in the casket: "Lincoln's complexion had always been dark, but now instead of being even darker, it was unpleasantly lighter, a grayish putty color. Around his mouth he still had the faintly happy expression that those who watched him die saw come over his face a few minutes after he stopped breathing.

"The trouble was that the smile had frozen on a face that was unfamiliar in its unresponsive stoniness. Gone was the mobility that so entranced anyone who had watched him in life: the magic lighting-up of the features had made a plain man handsome when his mind struck sparks."

The body, for better or worse, would be accompanied throughout the train journey by an Honor Guard. Many other passengers would rotate with the various stops of the Lincoln Funeral Train. Military and government leaders would routinely board at strategic points and depart further down the route at other points.

The body itself would be frequently loaded off of the hearse car, and later loaded back on following various ceremonies at different locations. However, "the remains will continue always under the special charge of the officers and escort assigned by the War Department."

This was a rule that would be strongly enforced. No other group—anywhere—was allowed to handle the casket of President Lincoln except to accompany the Honor Guard.

The Honor Guard would sit with the remains "until they are consigned to their final resting place" in Springfield, Illinois.

Included in the Honor Guard were some of the most distinguished and high-ranking officers in the military at the time. They were:

Brigadier General B.D. Townsend, assistant adjutant general of the Secretary of War Edwin Stanton;

Brigadier General James A Ekin, deputy quartermaster general;

Brigadier General AB. Eaton, commissary general of subsistence;

Brevet Major General J.G. Barnard, Lieutenant Colonel of Engineers;

Brigadier General G. D. Ramsey, Ordnance Department;

Brigadier General A. P. Howe, Chief of Artillery;

Brevet Brigadier General D.C. McCallum, Superintendent of Military Roads;

Major General D. Hunter, U.S. Volunteers.

Already the War Department had put forth a wealth of rules and regulations regarding the Lincoln Funeral Train.

First, the ruling military made it clear that the nation's entire railway system, for the purposes of this special trip, would be firmly and totally under military control. In effect, all existing railways ceased to be civilian for the remainder of the Lincoln Train journey and were indeed part of the military operation.

That particular and enormous railway control would rest with Brigadier General McCallum, a member of the Honor Guard. Gen. McCallum had directed the Union military railroad system during the Civil War.

And there were no exceptions anywhere along the line. According to military directives issued at the time, "all persons disobeying the orders shall be known to have violated military orders of the War Department, and shall be dealt with accordingly."

The military extended restrictions already in place to further restrict access to the Lincoln Funeral Train itself. Only authorized persons would be allowed entrance, and the number of persons actually allowed passage on the train from one location to another would be even more restricted.

Further, the military allowed that different engines from the various railway companies would be interchanged as the train proceeded on its journey. However, the train itself would not exceed nine cars, including the baggage car and the hearse car. Nevertheless, there were some provisions for additional sleeping cars under special circumstances.

In addition, Secretary Stanton had earlier in the week appointed the Illinois governor, John Brough, and John W. Garrett to act on a Committee of Arrangements in regard to the detailed schedule of transporting the remains of President Lincoln ultimately to Springfield.

"They (Brough and Garrett) are authorized to arrange the time tables with the respective railroad companies, do and regulate all things for safe and appropriate transportation," the Stanton declaration concluded.

The so-called time card they provided for the journey actually not only involved the larger cities like Baltimore, New York, Cleveland, and Chicago, but it also involved all the other cities, towns, and nearly obscure locations. There were hundreds of them.

Very ambitious, the time card spelled out specific times of arrival and departure for not only the major cities, but everywhere else in between as well. Generally, the idea was to retrace the grand route traveled by President Lincoln coming from Springfield to Washington for his first inauguration in 1861. Officially, it would be retracing with the "exception of two points," which was Pittsburgh and Cincinnati. The chief concern about Cincinnati was the unpredictability of Confederate sympathizers known in that region as Copperheads.

To guard against "accidents and detentions," it was decreed that the Lincoln Funeral Train go no faster than 20 miles per hour. Generally, the preferred speed was five miles per hour, slowing even more for mourners who were gathered along the sides of the track. As it would turn out, the train often just stopped for unexpectedly large crowds of spectators that appeared all along the nearly 1,700-mile journey.

The Transportation Committee confirmed what the War Department had already decreed, that "the special train, in all cases, have the right of road, and that all other trains be kept out of the way."

Moreover, they assured that a pilot or scout train engine would be kept running about ten minutes in advance of the funeral train. The pilot train would be equipped with lights (red by day and white by night) to signal a warning back to the funeral train should there be some sort of hazard. The pilot train also carried two armed guards, although there was little else in terms of security for such a massive journey.

More specifics of the Transportation Committee's announcement also provided for the number of cars in the train, but allowed for exceptions. The committee's regulations provided that at any time the funeral train went beyond midnight, or, as it was planned in Indianapolis, that it begins after midnight—at least two sleeping cars could be added, "and a greater number if the road can command them, sufficient for the accommodation of the escort."

They also ordered that two officers of the existing United States Military Railway Service be immediately dispatched "over the route to confer with several railway officers" and make all necessary arrangements for the funeral train's ultimate journey.

There was also generous use of the most modem day invention—the telegraph.

The telegraph was a major and massive tool as the Civil War came to an end and it was a ready one for the federal government in April of 1865. By mid-day of the day before the Lincoln Funeral Train was to depart Washington, the telegraph had been used to its ultimate.

Newspapers and their readers knew that Lincoln's assassin was actor John Wilkes

Booth, and that he had been injured in his leap to the stage of the Ford Theatre; and he was now being aided by a number of accomplices and accessories as he sought to escape through the country. They also knew of the Lincoln funeral and much of the details of the dramatic train journey across several states. Train stations had also been notified of the "time card" for the Lincoln Funeral Train and personnel had carefully posted the schedules in public places.

At about 6 a.m. on the morning of April 21, members of Lincoln's cabinet and especially invited guests assembled in the rotunda of the Capitol building in Washington. Congress was not in session during this tragic week; therefore, only a relatively few were represented there that morning.

At twenty minutes before 7 a.m., the coffin bearing the remains of the President was moved by twelve smartly dressed military sergeants and placed in the horse-drawn hearse that was waiting quietly in front of the Capitol.

A procession of noted officials was formed and in turn it slowly escorted the President's body to the depot of the Baltimore and Ohio Railroad Company on New Jersey Avenue. The darkly draped funeral train stood waiting. Most of those passengers who would accompany the body on its journey to a final resting place were already aboard. Several thousand soldiers positioned along the track that stretched from the depot would move to presentation of arms when the train slowly moved out.

This eye-witness account described the departing scene: "A portion of the soldiers in line near the depot were two regiments of US. Colored Troops. They stood with arms reversed, heads bowed, all weeping like children at the lost of a father. Their grief was of such undoubted sincerity as to effect the whole vast multitude.

"Dignified Governors of States, grave Senators, and scar-worn army officers, who had passed through scenes of blood and carnage unmoved, lost their self control and were melted to tears in the presence of such unaffected sorrow."

At 8 a.m., just on schedule, the Lincoln Funeral Train left Washington behind forever.

Company of U.S. Colored Infantry stationed in Washington, D.C. Photograph by Mathew Brady, ca. 1863. *Library of Congress photograph.*

Northward

(Maryland, Pennsylvania, New Jersey)

*"Here the people were not counted by
the thousands, but by acres."*

—Description of Philadelphia from
the Lincoln Funeral Train

The first direction of the Lincoln Funeral Train would be northward. Its schedule would call for the train to travel through Maryland, Pennsylvania, and New Jersey. Its mission was clear: allow as many people as possible just to see it passing.

It would take two hours for the train to reach its first major city, a 10 a.m. stop at Baltimore. That would leave enough time to once again review the committee's official rules and regulations:

1. The figures in the Table represent the time upon which the Pilot Engine has to run, and the funeral train will follow, leaving each station ten minutes behind the figures of this table.

2. The funeral train will pass stations at a speed not exceeding five miles an hour, the engineman tolling his bell as the train passers through the station and town.

3. Telegraph offices upon the entire route will be kept open during the passage of the funeral train, and as soon as the train has passed a station the operator will at once give notice to that effect to the next telegraph station.

4. The pilot engine will pass no telegraph station without first getting information of the funeral train having passed the last preceding telegraph station, coming to a full stop for that information, if necessary.

5. Upon the entire route a safety signal will be shown at each switch and bridge, and at entrance upon each curve, indicating that all is safe for the passage of pilot and train—each man in charge of a signal knowing personally such to be the case, so far as his foresight can provide it. The signal until reaching broad daylight, to be a white light, and from that point, a white flag, draped.

6. The engineman in charge of the pilot engine will carry two red lights in the night, and an American flag, draped, during the daylight, indicating that a train is following, and will also provide themselves with red lights, flags and extra men, to give immediate notice to the funeral train, in case of meeting with anything on the route causing delay or detention.

7. The engineman in charge of the funeral train will keep a sharp lookout for the pilot engine and its signals.

8. The pilot and funeral train will have the entire right to the line during its passage, and all engines and trains of every description will be kept out of the way.

9. Each road forming the route will run its train upon its own standard time."

Abraham Lincoln

Vintage postcard image of President Abraham Lincoln.

The story was the same at Branchville, Fort Meade, and Annapolis Junction. Over and over the great train had to slow or even briefly stop to acknowledge the increasing numbers of people who had appeared on the scene to see the Lincoln Special.

By contrast, Baltimore was more or less predictable. It was the first major stop scheduled for the train. It was the first time outside of Washington that the body of President Lincoln would be removed from the train. A waiting throng of more than 10,000 in Baltimore would be the first to view the remains.

While the April rain had held off in Baltimore, the sky was gray and overcast. The weather had certainly not deterred the growing numbers of people who now flooded the city.

In February of 1861 President-elect Lincoln had passed through the Camden Station in Baltimore on the way to Washington, D.C., where he was to be inaugurated as President. Lincoln had also changed trains at the Camden Station in November of 1863 en route to Gettysburg, Pennsylvania, to deliver what would become the legendary Gettysburg Address.

Once again, in April of 1864, Lincoln made an overnight visit to Baltimore and Camden Station for a speaking engagement in the city. Now, little more than a year later, the train arrived at the Camden Station on the Northern Central Railway's Baltimore-Harrisburg Line.

The plan was to drive the train straight through to Baltimore without "stoppage" in between.

Yet the crowds along the way were unexpected.

Places like Brentwood, Hyattsville, and Alexandria Junction had become gathering locations for great numbers of mourners who stood alongside the track as the Lincoln Funeral Train approached.

"As the train moved on to Camden Station in Baltimore," noted one observer, "thousands of Marylanders assembled by the way-side to catch a glimpse of the car which contained the corpse of the deceased President."

Signature of President Lincoln, endorsement reading, "Respectfully submitted to the Attorney General/A. Lincoln/ March 26, 1862." Framed. *Skinner, Inc.* estimated $3,000–$5,000.

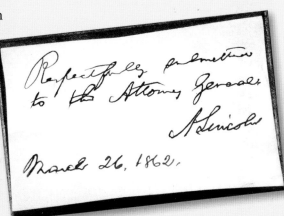

It was 10 a.m.

Despite the seemingly generous turnout of the public, there were concerns by those in charge of the train.

For one thing, this had been the city where, just four years before, Lincoln had hurried along in disguise for fear of harm. However, as one correspondent has written, "the place where he once feared assassination, now received his remains with every possible demonstration of respect."

Moreover, the city of Baltimore had at one time been the hometown of accused assassin John Wilkes Booth. Just days before the arrival of the Lincoln Funeral Train, the "hometown" city had posted a $10,000 reward for the arrest of Booth. City officials hoped the message was clear.

And so all went peacefully at the first scheduled stop of the funeral train, according to one account, because it, "was under the control of loyal men, who felt deeply grieved that a plot had been laid there (Baltimore) for his destruction when on his way to assume duties of his office; and they suffered still greater mortification that it was a native of their own city who had plunged the nation into mourning by the horrid crime of assassinating the President."

There was a salvo of artillery fire, but it was a planned part to mark the arrival of the late president.

Embossed vintage postcard of martyred President and lady with American flag. $8–$10.

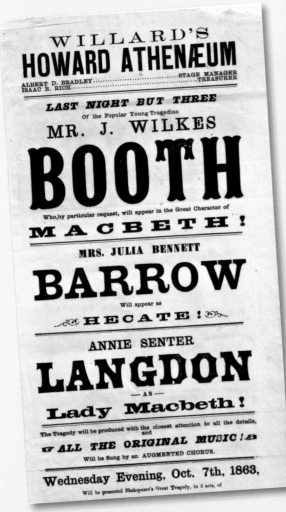

WILLARD'S
HOWARD ATHENÆUM
ALBERT D. BRADLEY..................STAGE MANAGER
ISAAC B. RICH..................TREASURER

LAST NIGHT BUT THREE
Of the Popular Young Tragedian

MR. J. WILKES

BOOTH

Who, by particular request, will appear in the Great Character of

MACBETH !

MRS. JULIA BENNETT

BARROW

Will appear as

HECATE !

ANNIE SENTER

LANGDON

—AS—

Lady Macbeth !

The Tragedy will be produced with the closest attention to all the details, and

ALL THE ORIGINAL MUSIC !
Will be Sung by an AUGMENTED CHORUS.

Wednesday Evening, Oct. 7th, 1863,
Will be presented Shakspeare's Great Tragedy, in 5 acts, of

Broadside featuring Maryland native and nationally known actor J. Wilkes Booth at a Boston theatre. It advertised Booth's performance in *Macbeth* during October of 1863. Approximately six by eighteen inches. *Skinner, Inc.*

At any rate the body of Lincoln was escorted from the train depot by an "immense procession" to the rotunda of the Merchants' Exchange, where it was placed on a "gorgeous" catafalque beautifully surrounded by flowers.

It was an impressive sight. The catafalque stood immediately beneath the dome of the building. It consisted of a raised dais, said to be eleven feet by four feet at the base. From the four corners rose "graceful columns" supporting a majestic cornice ornamented with silver stars.

The canopy itself rose to a point some 14 feet from the ground, and it was terminated in clusters of black plumes. Further, the whole structure was "richly" draped with black cloth. Some of the drape cloth, particularly those attached to the previously described four corners, was bordered with silver fringe.

Oddly enough, there were no actual ceremonies at the train station or in the rotunda of the Merchants' Exchange. There was public viewing of the body, however; first by ranking officials, and later by the general public gathered in large numbers outside of the structure.

Elsewhere in Baltimore, streets with immediate access to the Merchants' Exchange were crowded with citizens from before dawn who are hoping to view the remains or at least take part in a funeral procession. One account described it as "so great (in numbers) that it was almost impossible to move on any of the foot walks surrounding the buildings."

"Work was suspended," reported one correspondent, "the hum of traffic was hushed; all turned aside from their usual avocations to unite in the observation of the day, and in paying reverence to the departed."

At exactly 2:30 p.m., "to the regret of thousands," the coffin bearing Lincoln's remains was closed, and the honor guard escorted it to the waiting hearse. At that time, the public procession was more or less re-formed and took up what was described as

"its mournful march" back—not to Camden Station, but to the depot of a different railroad company, Northern Central Railway Company.

Regarding the departure at the depot, one observer noted the firing of guns at the station in tribute to the President and the marked "sorrows of a people who felt that the Republic had indeed lost its best friend."

Next were more places and people along the countryside of Maryland.

The Lincoln Funeral Train left Baltimore promptly at 3 p.m. that Friday afternoon and arrived at Cockeyville just one hour later, after passing through more than a half-dozen Maryland locations. At every site there were significant gatherings of townsfolk and perhaps travelers.

At around 4:20 p.m. the train passed through Phoenix, Maryland, and continued northward toward the state line of Maryland and Pennsylvania.

This was the schedule for Maryland:

(FRIDAY, APRIL 21, 1865)
Brentwood
Hyattesville
Alexandria Junction
College Park
Berwyn
Branchville
Beltsville
Ammendale
Muirkirk
Contee
Laurel
Savage
Fort Meade
Jessups
Dorseys
Annapolis Junction
Hanover Station
Relay Station
St. Denis
Camnden
Baltimore (Camden Station) arrive 10 a.m. depart 3 p.m.
Ruxton
Procton (Riderwood)

Mt. Washington

Hollis

Lutherville

Timonium

Pandora

Texas

Cockeyville arrive at 4 p.m.

Ashland

Phoenix arrive at 4:20 p.m.

Sparks

Glencoe

Corbett

Moneton

Blue Mount

White Hall

Graystone

Parkiton

Walkers Switch

Just over the Pennsylvania state line the train was joined by Major General George Cadwalader. General Cadwalader, a native of Philadelphia, boarded the train under a special order of the War Department issued earlier, which provided that various high-ranking generals be aboard to coordinate efforts with state and local authorities.

The distinguished General had served both during the previous Mexican-American War and the Civil War. At one point, Cadwalader had commanded some of the forces of the Army of Shenandoah. Ultimately, he became commander of the Pennsylvania force of the United States Volunteers, and he held that post when he came aboard the funeral train.

General Cadwalader would remain coordinating commander on the train until relieved at the New Jersey state line by General John Adams Dix.

At around 6:50 p.m. on the same Friday evening, the train pulled into the station at York, Pennsylvania.

It was a brief stop, but six ladies "dressed in black, were kindly permitted to enter the funeral car and place upon the Lincoln coffin a beautiful wreath of white rose, camellias, and other rare flowers."

Another York account noted of the women, "Silently they performed their last tribute to the illustrious patriot, and when they retired from the car there were no dry eyes among the military chieftains who stood guard over the bier."

The funeral train arrived for its next stop at the Pennsylvania state capital of Harrisburg, Pennsylvania, during an intense thunderstorm around 8:30 p.m. that same Friday. Despite bolts of lightning and heavy rain, crowds of people lined the city's streets from the depot all the way to the Capitol building itself.

Harrisburg mayor William Roumfort had earlier proclaimed, "all business houses and drinking saloons were to be closed during the stay of the funeral cortege."

Despite the heavy rain, more than 1,500 soldiers stood in tribute to President Lincoln under the command of Colonel Thomas S. Mather. They had been standing in place for hours before the funeral cortege finally arrived.

Among the many in uniform at Harrisburg was Lt. William Bogardus, an Ohio native who was then an officer of the 24th U.S. Colored Regiment.

He later wrote in his diary of the scene:

"On the 21st I was in the City...judging by the looks of all the houses everybody in the city has lost a friend. All the houses, stores, public buildings, and hotels are draped in mourning.

"We go to escort the body from the depot to the State House where it rests in state until Monday. As we passed the coffin I gave the last salute to him I ever shall. It was my privilege to salute him often while living.

"The procession was five miles long. The hearse is drawn by six black horses. Some people remained in line 24 hours."

The body was moved to the State Capitol and placed in the hall of the House of Representatives "amid emblems of sorrow, and surrounded by a circle of white flowering almonds."

The Lincoln Funeral Train at the station in Harrisburg, Pennsylvania, the decorated and guarded funeral car bearing the body of President Lincoln. *Prints and Photographs Division, Library of Congress.*

Under the command of Colonel Mather, a military and civic procession began forming at 8 a.m. on the following Saturday morning there in Harrisburg. According to one observer there, "The remains were escorted through the principal streets to the depot. In order to have as much daylight as possible for the later procession in Philadelphia, the train moved from Harrisburg at 11 a.m. (Saturday)—one hour before schedule time."

Actually other accounts had the funeral train leaving Harrisburg slightly later than that time, but several reports noted that at locations immediately beyond Harrisburg were "thousands of men, women, and children assembled at depots and along the line of the railway, to pay respect to the services and the memory of the patriot around whom their affections and their hopes had clustered."

At Middleton, Elizabethtown, Mount Joy, Landisville, and Dillerville in particular, one correspondent observed, "In many places insignia of sorrow were displayed, and all seemed anxious to obtain a passing view of the mournful cortege."

Every place of business was closed in the Pennsylvania town of Lancaster when the funeral train finally stopped there shortly after 1 p.m. on Saturday, April 22.

"At the outskirts of the town a large force of the Lancaster Iron Works lined the road, their buildings all draped in mourning," an observer later wrote. A short distance further down the Lancaster line the narrative continued, "It was affecting to see old men who had been carried in their chairs and seated beside the track, and women with infants in their arms, assembled to look at the passing cortege."

At least 20,000 people were standing in the massive crowd when the train finally stopped at the Lancaster depot. The depot itself was "artistically" decorated with American flags and black crepe. At the side of the depot was a large sign that read:

"Abraham Lincoln, the Illustrious Martyr of Liberty, the nation mourns his loss; though dead, he still lives."

Lancaster was also well known as the hometown of former President James Buchanan. President Buchanan had served a single term immediately before President Lincoln. While Lincoln was in the White House, Buchanan was living more or less in retirement in Lancaster.

Witnesses said that Buchanan was in his carriage on the outskirts of the multitude of people when the Lincoln Funeral Train passed through Lancaster. Meanwhile, another noted resident of that community, fiery Congressional leader Thaddeus Stevens, was also found to be watching the train.

According to reports, Stevens was standing on a rock, entirely alone, under a bridge the funeral train passed over. One witness aboard the train said Stevens seemed absorbed in silent meditation, unaware that he was being observed. When the actual hearse car approached, he reverently uncovered his head, and replaced his hat as the train moved away.

Stevens and United States Senator Charles Sumner were the prime leaders of the Radical Republicans during the Civil War and the following Reconstruction Era. Stevens was a major backer of the 14th Amendment, which provided citizenship to former slaves, and the 1867 Reconstruction Acts, which divided the South into five military districts controlled by martial law.

Signed one-page document regarding the appointment of Frank Bell as Captain in the Pennsylvania Reserve Volunteers Corps. It is signed by President Lincoln and countersigned by Secretary of War Edwin Stanton. It is dated 1863. Bell was in Company 1, the McKean Rifles from McKean County. The document contained some fold separations and toning. *Skinner, Inc.* estimated $3,500–$4,500.

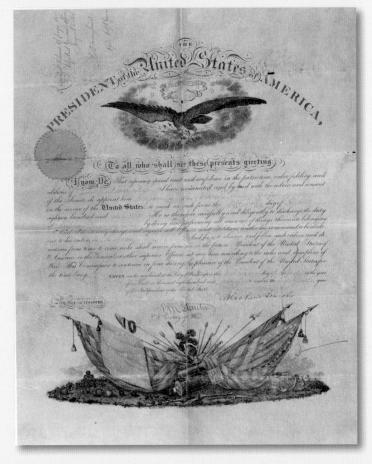

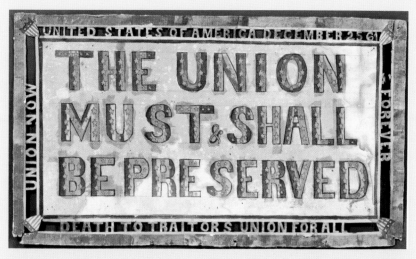

Pro-Union painted and cutwork sign, early 1860s. The center of the sign is painted in patriotic colors with the inscription, "The Union Must & Shall Be Preserved." In smaller letters is "Death to Traitors/Union For All." The sign is about 13 by 22 inches in a wooden frame. *Skinner, Inc.*, estimated $1,500–$2,500.

The flamboyant and controversial Stevens, from Pennsylvania's Eighth District, was later portrayed by movie star Tommy Lee Jones in the 2012 film *Lincoln,* produced by Steven Spielberg. The movie was based on the best-selling book *Team of Rivals* by Doris Kerns Goodwin.

As the train came within miles of the great city of Philadelphia, there were unbroken columns of people on each side of the railroad. The lines were almost solid for mile after mile nearing the population center.

At West Philadelphia observers reported residents flocking across Market Street by the hundreds, "while the Camden ferryboats apparently brought across the Delaware (River) about one half of the population of New Jersey."

When the train finally rolled into the city of Philadelphia, the scene was unbelievable.

About a half-million people stood on the streets awaiting the train. After days of preparation, the great numbers were formed in marching order for the funeral

Lincoln Funeral Train as it appeared in the city of Philadelphia, Pennsylvania, in April of 1865. *Prints and Photographs Division, Library of Congress.*

The hearse shown here is carrying the casket of President Lincoln through the city streets of Philadelphia, Pennsylvania. Soldiers are just in front of a huge crowd of mourners. *Prints and Photographs Division, Library of Congress.*

procession—some four to 12 abreast. The grand procession would include 11 divisions, accounting for every organization in the city, both military and civic.

From a distance the wide line of the procession extended out for more than seven miles.

"Here," proclaimed one observer on the majestic scene, "the people were not counted by the thousands, but by the acres."

The train had actually arrived in the city of Philadelphia between 4:30 p.m. and 4:50 p.m. depending on which source was keeping the most accurate time. At any rate, the train had arrived about an hour ahead of its previously scheduled time.

At last, the procession, with the remains of President Lincoln on an elaborately

black-decorated hearse, began to press forward.

"It moved through the wide and beautiful streets of this city to the sound of solemn music, by a great number of bands," wrote one correspondent. "The insignia of sorrow seemed to be on every house. The poor testified their grief by displaying such emblems as their limited means could command, and the rich, more profuse, not because of their sorrow as greater, but because their wealth enabled them to manifest it on a larger scale."

It was nearing 8 p.m. in the evening when the procession finally arrived at the entrance of Independence Hall. At that point, the Union League Association took charge and conveyed the casket to a platform in the

Railroad workers and others stand alongside the Lincoln Funeral Train that had stopped in the city of Philadelphia while passing through the state of Pennsylvania. Vintage postcard, estimated $25–$50.

center of the great Hall. The head of the body was placed close to the pedestal on which the old Liberty Independence stood. This was the bell that had rung out the nation's independence on the Fourth of July in 1776.

One observer later described the spectacle as the casket lay in historic Independence Hall that evening:

"The interior of the Hall has been covered on many occasions, but never before had such skill and taste been displayed as on this occasion. The scene was a combination of enchantment and gloom of unexampled brilliancy and splendor.

"Evergreens and flowers of rare fragrance and beauty were placed around the coffin. At the head were various bouquets, at the feet were burning tapers. The walls were hung with portraits of many great and good patriots, soldiers and civilians, who have long since passed away."

President-elect Lincoln had been one of the "great and good" patriots who had spoken there. While en route to Washington in 1861, he had delivered a moving message to those in attendance about saving the Union. It was also about the liberty promised in the Declaration of Independence.

"But, if this country cannot be saved without giving up that principle, I was about to say, I would rather be assassinated upon this spot than to surrender it."

President Lincoln signed this manuscript granting 160 acres of land to Jehiel Jones for his service in the Vermont Militia during the War of 1812. The document is dated September 15, 1864. Complete with official wax seal, and framed, it is 16 inches by 10 inches. *Skinner, Inc.*, estimated $4,000–$6,000.

Still, under the circumstances, the mood of the great crowd was somber and relatively well-behaved. One account described the masses of people as one where "little disorder prevailed, every one apparently being deeply impressed with the great solemnity of the occasion."

Observers said that once a person stepped into line it took another four to five hours before entrance into the Hall was possible. Spectators were not allowed to stop beside President Lincoln's coffin, but were kept moving forward after a brief glance at the remains. Even so the great numbers in waiting continued to steadily but orderly push ahead.

A report of that day's events later published by the *Philadelphia Inquirer* offered similar praise:

"A grand, emphatic and unmistakable tribute of affectionate devotion to the memory of our martyred chief was that paid by Philadelphia on the arrival of his (Lincoln's) remains on Saturday evening.

"No mere love of excitement, no idle curiosity to witness a splendid pageant, but a feeling far deeper, more earnest, and founded in infinitely nobler sentiments, must have inspired that throng, which, like the multitudinous waves of a swelling seas, surged along our streets from every corner of the city, gathering in a dense, impenetrable mass along the route prescribed for the procession."

It also spoke glowingly of the pre-arrival crowds:

"The myriads of expectant faces gathering around the depot at Broad and Prime streets, and lining the route of the procession for hours before the arrival of the funeral train; the various civic associations marching in orderly columns with banners draped in mourning..."

American flags were proudly displayed all along the route of the Lincoln Funeral Train. They varied from hand-held stars and strips to huge examples on buildings, and even those once used by the military in actual battles. This Pennsylvania 53rd Volunteer Regiment silk flag had been earlier awarded to a severely wounded soldier. The Potter County solider had been discharged some months before the death of President Lincoln. *Skinner, Inc.*, estimated value of 23.5 by 21.5 inch flag, $8,000–$12,000.

United States black soldiers at Camp William Penn near Philadelphia, Pennsylvania. Distinguished "Colored" troops from here took part in President Lincoln's funeral ceremonies at Washington, and later others carried the Lincoln casket during funeral services at Philadelphia. The 13-acre camp just northwest of Philadelphia in Cheltenham Township trained more than 10,000 African-American soldiers during the course of the war. This chromolithograph recruiting poster was issued in 1863. *Swan Galleries*, estimated value $8,000–$12,000.

Columns began forming around 1 a.m. Monday morning to begin the procession that would return the casketed remains from Independence Hall to the train depot. The coffin was officially closed around 2 a.m.

The returning escort included the 187th Pennsylvania Infantry, the various city troops, the guard of honor, and a special detachment of soldiers and firefighters assigned to guard the body. A band also played music along the march. The procession reached the Kensington railway station around 4 a.m. that morning and the funeral train departed shortly afterwards.

At the state line near Morrisville, Pennsylvania, there was an exchange of officials and other dignitaries. Joining the group were the Rev. D. Henry Miller, New Jersey Governor W. Parker, and United States Senator John P. Stockton. Departing was Pennsylvania Governor G. Curtin, among others.

This was the schedule for Pennsylvania:

(FRIDAY, APRIL 21, 1865)
New Freedom arrive 5:30 p.m.
Glen Rock
Hanover Junction (Smysar)
Shrewsbury arrive 6:30 p.m.
York arrive 6:50 p.m.
Emigsville
Mount Wolf
Wago Junction
York Haven (Cly)
Goldsboro
Enola

Summerdale
Rockville
Harrisburg arrive 8:30 p.m.

(SATURDAY, APRIL 22, 1865)
Harrisburg depart 11:15 a.m.
Lochtel
Baldwin
High Spire
White House
Middletown
Intersection
Hillsdale
Conewago
Elizabethtown
Rheem's
Springville
Mount Joy
Salunga
Landisville
Kauffmann's
Dillerville
Lancaster arrive 1:05 p.m.
Bird-In-Hand
Leaman Place
Hillsdale
Kinzers
Gap
Christina
Penningtonville
Parkersburg arrive 2:15 p.m.
Pomeroy
Coatsville arrive 2:30 p.m.
Caln
Thorbdale
Gallagrerville
Downingtown
Doobine
Oakland
White Land
Steam Boat
Garrett
Frazer
Paoli
Reeseville
Eagle
Berwyn
Wayne

Morgan's Corner
Radnor
Villa Nova
Rosemont
Bryn Mawr
Haverford
Ardmore
Athensville
Wynnewood
Elmo
Merion
Overbrook
Hestonville
Mantua
West Philadelphia
Philadelphia (Kensington Station)
arrive 4:50 p.m.

(MONDAY, APRIL 24, 1865)
Philadelphia depart 4 a.m.
Bridesburg
Wissinoming
Tacony
Holmsburg
Penny PO
Pierson's
Torresdale
Bories
Andalusia
Cornwell's
Eddington
Schenck
Bristol arrive at 5 a.m.
Old Pring
Tully Town
Wheat Sheaf
Penn Valley
Morrisville

Prominent passenger Senator Stockton was a passenger steeped in controversy, yet he had been in the U.S. Senate little more than a month. Eventually he would anger a significant number of fellow senators by voting against the 14th Amendment, which offered civil liberties to freed slaves and harsh sanctions to Confederate states.

Historic letter from the Head Quarters Armies of the United States, March 30, 1865, to Secretary of War Edwin Stanton from President Lincoln. It reads in part, "I begin to feel that I ought to be at home, and yet I dislike to leave without seeing nearer to the end of General Grant's present movement." Later the President writes of battle at Petersburg, "The sound was distinct here, as also were the flashes of the guns up in the clouds. It seemed to me a great battle, but the older hands here scarcely noticed it…" Lincoln had gone there a few days before his assassination, to consult with Grant. *Skinner, Inc.*, estimated $35,000–$50,000.

In retaliation, the senators voted, by a majority of one, to unseat Senator Stockton. It was a questionable vote since the U.S. Constitution specified that a two-thirds majority was necessary to unseat a U.S. Senator. As a countermeasure, the U.S. Senate claimed that Stockton was being unseated retroactively, (before becoming an official member) and thus under a different expulsion measure.

The state of New Jersey would be outraged at Stockton's removal. They were so outraged that they would rescind their earlier ratification of the 14th Amendment in protest. Eventually Stockton returned to the U.S. Senate and served a full six-year term.

But on this April day in 1865 Senator Stockton was riding the Lincoln Funeral Train.

Promptly at 5:30 a.m. the Lincoln Special crossed the Delaware River passing officially from the state of Pennsylvania to the state of New Jersey.

"As the draped cars passed through New Jersey," noted one observer, "the people of that state evinced the same grief, and paid the same honors to the funeral train as it had hitherto been done by the people of Maryland and Pennsylvania."

Bells were tolling in the city of Trenton as the train rolled to a stop there. "Every hilltop on the line of the road, and other advantageous points," noted one report, "were occupied with throngs of spectators."

Meanwhile, a group had formed in front of the depot to pay formal tribute to President Lincoln. It was described this way by an eyewitness: "A detachment of the Reserved Veteran and Invalid Corps, drawn up in line on the platform, gave the customary funeral honors. Music was performed by an instrumental band, minute guns were fired, and the bells continued to toll. Everywhere the emblems of mourning were prominent."

Interestingly, of the entire train trip Trenton was the only state capital where the train did not stop for full funeral services. It did halt however for the recognition of some 20,000 people standing in vicinity.

One correspondent later noted, "Its (Trenton) location between two great cities, (Philadelphia and New York City), so near them, is, no doubt, the cause of its being made an exception."

The funeral train arrived at New Brunswick at about 7:30 a.m. that same morning and halted there for about 30 minutes before a large crowd of mourners. There were brief prayers and hymns as the train departed heading northward.

Near the Elizabeth station a group of young men displayed banners, each bearing a single word and the usual crepe attachments. Words viewed from aboard the train were "Victory," "Peace," "Union," "Grant," and "Sherman."

At Newark the private residences and public buildings and stores and workshops were all elaborately draped in mourning. Bells were of course tolling, and guns were fired. Elsewhere, the United States Hospital in the Newark area was finely decorated in mourning drapes. Many soldiers on crutches were bravely formed in a line there near the hospital.

This report from an observer:

"All of Newark, with the exception of those at the windows, seemed to be out of doors. Trees and housetops, doorsteps and car-trucks—in fact, all the highest attainable positions and points where an unobstructed view could be had, were occupied."

There sights of men and women shedding tears, and of people from all stations in life standing silently at the vision of the remarkable Lincoln Funeral Train.

A few days later a young man in the crowd that day wrote to "Grandma" about the event in Newark.

"There was a great procession here..., the funeral of the President, it was very large, indeed the largest I heard that ever paraded in Newark, I only saw part of it however... The body of the President is to be in New York on Monday and I would like very much to go and see him for I never saw him when alive, but I think there will be such a crowd that one would get crushed to death almost just as it was at the Duke of Wellington's funeral in London...

Mr. Geo. A Keen has gone to Richmond and if he wants to get home right away I fear (he) will have some difficulty because they are so fearful the murderer of the late President may escape. They are omitting no pains to capture him and I am sure I hope they will if any ever deserved to forfeit his life he does..."

Meanwhile, as the train departed that city, a passenger noted the lingering view from the train. "For more than a mile, those on the train could only perceive one sea of human beings," commented a passenger writing of the stop in Newark later.

At Jersey City, the train arrived at about 10 a.m. that morning. Far above the train, however, the station clock was stopped at 7:20 a.m.—what was believed to be the time when President Lincoln was pronounced dead in the boarding house across from Ford's Theatre.

Elsewhere in Jersey City bells were typically ringing and cannons were booming. Those aboard the train disembarked as the casket was moved along to a nearby building and its platform. Shortly there was singing from a vast choir composed of German musical associations in the gallery of the building.

Officially it was here at Jersey City that General Cadwalader would be relieved by arriving General John Dix. Dix was commander of the military department of New York, and he would travel with the cortege through the entire length of New York and across the northern tip of Pennsylvania.

General Dix has served as U.S. Secretary of the Treasury under President James Buchanan; prior to that, he had been a United States Senator serving the state of New York. Dix was best remembered during the outbreak of the Civil War for a famous telegram to Treasury agents stationed in New Orleans. It read, "If anyone attempts to haul down the American flag, shoot him on the spot." The telegram was intercepted by Confederates and never actually delivered to Treasury agents, but it made Dix a legend.

The passage through New Jersey initially did not include as many formal stops as had been planned for Pennsylvania, for example.

But everywhere the turnout was greater than planners had anticipated.

Again an observer on the Lincoln Funeral Train commented as it departed the state of New Jersey:

"At so many points where non-stoppage was expected, entire neighborhoods, old and young, men and women, the latter frequently with children in their arms, turned out by the roadside by night and day, and anxiously watched the gorgeous funeral train as it passed."

Later in the day, still at Jersey City, the body of President Lincoln was taken on a departing ferry across the Hudson River and on to New York City. The hearse rail car itself would be taken across same river on a separate ferry boat.

"As the remains were conveyed from the depot to the boat, the choir chanted a solemn dirge and continued on with it until the ferry boat reached the opposite side of the Hudson River," noted one account. "The shipping of all nations in the harbor displayed their flags at half-mast."

This was the schedule for New Jersey:

(MONDAY, APRIL 24, 1865)
    Trenton Junction arrive 5:45 a.m.
    Lawrence Station
    Princeton Junction arrive 6:45 a.m.
    Plainsboro
    Monmouth Junction
    Dean's
    Millstone Junction
    New Brunswick arrive 7:30 a.m.
    Piscataway
    Metuchen
    Union Town
    Houghtonville
    Rahway arrive 8:34 am.
    Linden
    Elizabeth arrive 8:45 a.m.
    Waverly Park
    Newark arrive 9:15 a.m.
    Jersey City arrive 10 a.m.

Westward

(New York)

With the waiting depot, the arriving coffin,
And somber faces,
With dirges through the night
With the thousand voices rising
Strong and solemn...

—Walt Whitman

Dark clouds offered the threat of rain by mid-morning in New York City.

Within the inner circle of planners for the Lincoln Funeral Train there were some concerns about the entry into the city. It was, of course, a bastion of the North, but it was capable of trouble and lawlessness as well.

Just two years earlier the city had erupted with rioting when federal authorities attempted the enforcement of the so-called Act for Enrolling and Calling Out of National Forces. For three days in 1863 mobs ruled the streets reeking rampage and wreckage throughout the city.

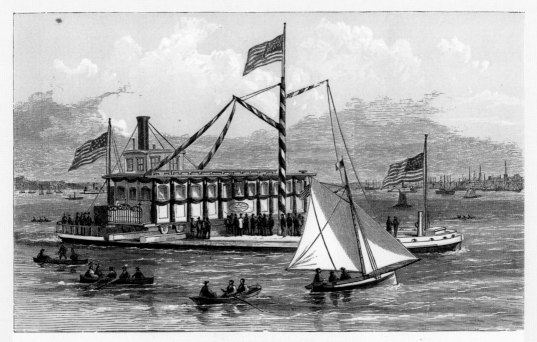

FUNERAL CAR CROSSING HUDSON RIVER.

Funeral car crossing the Hudson River by noted artist/journalist William Waud. This scene basically between New Jersey and New York was first depicted in *Harper's Weekly* and later in a special series of engravings. *Author's collection.*

EXECUTIVE MANSION,

Washington, D. C., July 2ᵈ 1863.

I, ABRAHAM LINCOLN, President of the United States of America, and Commander=in=chief of the Army and Navy thereof, having taken into consideration the number of volunteers and militia furnished by and from the several States, including the State of Massachusetts, and the period of service of said volunteers and militia since the commencement of the present rebellion, in order to equalize the numbers among the Districts of the said States, and having considered and allowed for the number already furnished as aforesaid, and the time of their service aforesaid, do hereby assign One thousand Nine Hundred and fifty-four as the first proportional part of the quota of troops to be furnished by the First DISTRICT OF THE STATE OF Massachusetts under this, the first call made by me on the State of Massachusetts, under the act approved March 3, 1863, entitled "An Act for Enrolling and Calling out the National Forces, and for other purposes," and, in pursuance of the act aforesaid, I order that a draft be made in the said First DISTRICT OF THE STATE OF Massachusetts for the number of men herein assigned to said District, and FIFTY PER CENT. IN ADDITION.

IN WITNESS WHEREOF, I have hereunto set my hand and caused the seal of the United States to be affixed.

Done at the City of Washington, this Second — day of July ——, in the year of our Lord one thousand eight hundred and sixty-three, and of the independence of the United States, the eighty-eighth. seventh.

Abraham Lincoln

The original letter may have been a factor in the New York City riots in 1863. It is concerning the first draft call for troops from Massachusetts, requesting 1,954 men "as the first proportional part of the quota of troops to be furnished of the state of Massachusetts." The document was the result of the passage of the Act for Enrolling and Calling Out of National Forces. The draft so enraged many of those in the North, according to some historians, it spawned the New York Draft riots in which mobs ruled the streets of New York for three days in 1863. *Skinner, Inc.*, realized auction price $18,800.

It was not without trepidation that the ferry boat with President Lincoln's remains landed at the base of Desbrosses Street in New York City. It was 10 a.m. on April 24, 1865. However, aside from occasional pickpockets there would be no problems in the great city.

From the edge of the water the coffin was moved to an especially prepared, glass-sided hearse at the edge of the street. The hearse itself was eight feet wide and extended 14 feet long. The platform of this majestic hearse car rose well above the ground. In the center of the platform was a dais where the coffin would be placed.

Above the dais was a canopy 15 feet high. It was in turn supported by columns and in part by a miniature temple of liberty. The canopy was given silver fringe and black cloth. Its corners each held rich plumes of black and white feathers. At the base of each column were three American flags slightly inclined outward and covered with black crepe. Meanwhile, the platform was covered with black cloth, which spilled from the sides

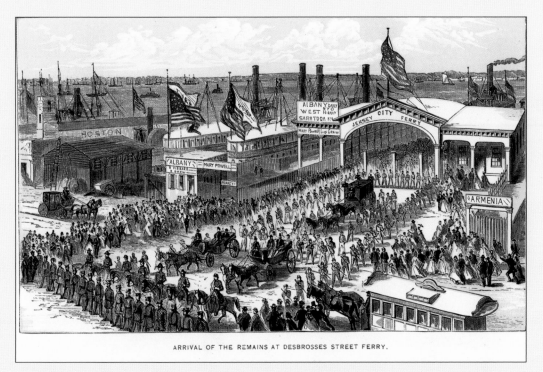

ARRIVAL OF THE REMAINS AT DESBROSSES STREET FERRY.

Arrival of President Lincoln's remains at Desbrosses Street in New York City, a sketch by William Waud. Waud covered the Civil War and the Lincoln funeral for *Harper's Weekly*. *Author's collection*.

nearly to the ground. It was further edged with silver bullion fringe.

The inside of the hearse car was lined with white satin and fluted.

At this height, five feet from the street, the coffin could clearly be seen by the crowds that stood by nearly motionless in awe of the sight.

Further, this grand hearse was to be drawn from its start at the base of Desbrosse Street by sixteen white horses, each horse covered with black trimming. Each horse would be led, in the procession, by its own individual groom.

Along the streets of New York City the procession moved slowly, escorted by the Seventh Regiment of the New York National Guard. It moved up Hudson Street, then to Canal Street, and then up Canal Street to mighty Broadway, and finally, down Broadway to the west gate of City Hall.

Elsewhere in New York City poet Walt Whitman had taken a ferry over the East River also headed toward Manhattan. As Whitman finally reached Broadway to witness the passing of the hearse and its growing procession, the dark clouds at last gave way to rain.

Later it prompted Whitman to describe ominous darkness overhead and the grim reality beneath it. "Black clouds driving overhead. Lincoln's death—black, black, black, as you look toward the sky—long broad black like great serpents."

Strikingly the funeral procession that followed the Lincoln hearse "was in keeping with the funeral car," noted one contemporary source, "the whole thing being indescribably grand and imposing."

The whole thing moved yet another observer to provide this narrative:

"As far as the eye could see, a dense mass of people, many of them wearing some insignia of mourning, filled the streets and crowded every window. The fronts of the houses were draped in mourning, and the national ensign (flag) displayed at half-mass from the top of almost every building.

PROCESSION PASSING FIFTH AVENUE HOTEL.

The Lincoln funeral procession passing Fifth Avenue in New York City as shown in an April 1865 drawing and later engraving. More of the work of William Waud, but unsigned. *Author's collection.*

VIEW OF THE CATAFALQUE IN FRONT OF CITY HALL.

A view of the Lincoln catafalque in front New York's City Hall as drawn by artist/journalist William Waud in April of 1865. This scene was later part of a series of engravings. *Author's collection.*

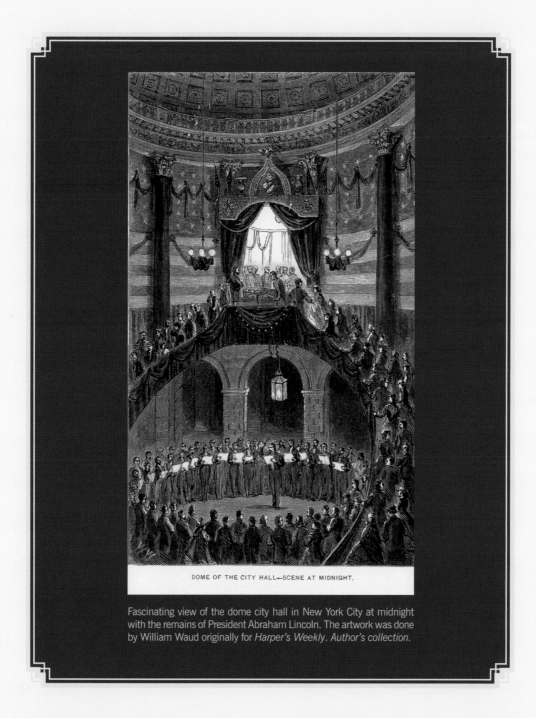

DOME OF THE CITY HALL—SCENE AT MIDNIGHT.

Fascinating view of the dome city hall in New York City at midnight with the remains of President Abraham Lincoln. The artwork was done by William Waud originally for *Harper's Weekly*. *Author's collection.*

"The procession was simply a dense mass of human beings."

As the massive assembly of humanity moved along in its growing grandeur with its now 18 bands thundering, guns were being fired from different locations, and bells were tolling from nearly every church steeple in New York City. The chimes high above Trinity Church loudly "wailed forth" the tune of Old Hundred in what was described as "a most solemn and impressive manner."

There was singing at City Hall as the casket was removed from the hearse and carefully carried into the rotunda. This time the singing

A look at the April 1865 obsequies of Abraham Lincoln in New York City. Drawing by noted Civil War artist William Waud. Of the set of eight New York City Lincoln Funeral drawings, this one bore the artist's initials W.W. *Author's collection.*

was the chanting of some 800 voices provided by a group specially selected for the occasion.

The Hall had of course been richly decorated for this remarkable event. The entire room that held the remains was draped in black. The center of the ceiling was dotted with silver stars relieved by black. The surrounding drapery was finished with heavy silver fringe, and the curtains of black velvet were also looped with silver fringe.

"The coffin rested on a raised dais, on an inclined plane, the inclination being such that the face of the departed patriot was in view of visitors while passing for two or three minutes each," wrote one correspondent.

Just before the public was allowed access, the two aforementioned embalmers who had accompanied the remains on the Lincoln Funeral Train had frantically rearranged the body. There were observations by some that the body "had been somewhat disturbed by the journey." Others might have been painfully aware that the state of the remains, nearly ten days since the death at this point, was frankly declining.

At any rate a portion of the casket was left open, as had been the case in other viewing stops, revealing a view of the upper portion of the breast and the face of Abraham Lincoln.

Beyond that however the casket itself was almost buried with rare and exotic floral coverings. A large military guard, in addition to the Honor Guard, stood nearby as the public began flowing into the area.

Public viewing was underway then "early the same afternoon, and from that time until 12 midnight. The next day, Tuesday, April 25th, a continuous stream passed through the Hall." Outside the hundreds of voices with the German musical societies of New York continued their moving requiem adding what one witness commented was, "the most thrilling effect."

Crowds line Broadway in New York City as the Lincoln Funeral procession with its horse-drawn carriages proceeds toward Union Square, in April of 1865. *Prints and Photographs Division, Library of Congress.*

President Lincoln's body is removed from the New York City Hall and placed in hearse funeral car. The drawing is dated April 25, 1865 and appeared in *Harper's Weekly* on May 13, 1865.

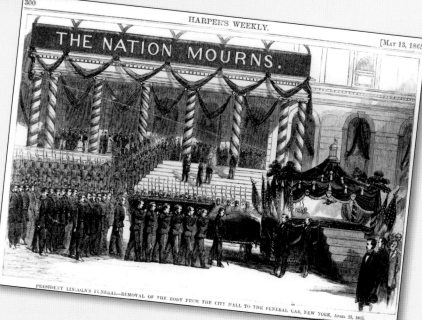

VIEW OF THE CITY HALL.

Grand and sweeping view of New York City Hall with the horses pulling the hearse of President Abraham Lincoln. A banner over the City Hall entrance reads, "The Nation Mourns." One of a series of drawings by William Waud, 1865. *Author's collection.*

Around 10 a.m. on that special Tuesday, the viewing was briefly halted for a ceremony involving highly regarded explorer Captain William Parker Snow and some rather odd relics to be interred in the Lincoln casket. The *New York Herald* later published this brief account of the event:

"Captain Parker Snow, the distinguished commander of the *Artie* and *Antarctic* exploring expeditions, presented to General Dix, with a view of being interred in the coffin of the President, some interesting relics of Sir John Franklin's ill-fated expedition.

"They consisted of a tattered leaf of a Prayer Book, on which the first word legible was the word Martyr, and a piece of fringe and some portions of a uniform. These suggestive relics, which are soon to be buried out of sight, were found in a boat lying under the head of a human skeleton."

Earlier in the 1850s it was Snow who claimed to a vision of the whereabouts of the missing Artic expedition of Sir Franklin. Financed by Lady Jane Franklin, Sir Franklin's widow, he explored the region without success. However, he later undertook various other expeditions, some more noteworthy than others.

Shortly after 11 a.m. on the same murky Tuesday, the coffin was closed, and another grand procession was formed.

"Notwithstanding such vast numbers that had viewed the corpse, there were thousands who had waited for hours, in the long lines, to obtain a look at the well-known face," offered a correspondent at the scene, "who were obliged to turn away sadly and be disappointed. This disappointment was not confined to any class or condition of men."

At this point one account details how dejected were the storied representatives of England, Russia, and France:

"They came in, glittering with scarlet, gold and silver lace, high coat collars, bearing embroidered clocked hats under their arms, with other costly trappings, and high birth and breeding in every gesture, desirous of seeing the corpse, but they were too late."

Like the common folk, the high-ranking foreign diplomats were turned away.

At half past noon, with the casket again in place the hearse complete again with sixteen white horses moved down Broadway and the farewell part of the funeral pageant had begun. It was led by a military force of 15,000 men, including the staffs of several brigades and divisions, with their batteries. Then came so-called civil societies or ethic and social groups, and other dignitaries, and then just great, great masses of people.

Ultimately it would become marching throngs moving shoulder-to-shoulder reaching about five miles in length. In the procession alone there were probably more than 60,000 people, all moving forward slowly as one.

The procession was dwarfed only by the immense crowds it passed.

One witness noted that the New York City streets were so jammed it was like "standing in a dense human hedge twelve or fifteen people deep."

Everywhere was an emblem of mourning or a simply worded sign in the crowd.

"Mourning emblems were displayed in the procession in such profusion as to be almost a wilderness of sable drapery," commented one witness, "and the mottoes and inscriptions on houses along the line of march, and those carried in the procession, would if collected, make of volume of themselves."

EXAMPLES:
"The workman dies, but the work goes on."
"His deeds have made his name immortal."
"Let others hail the rising sun,
We bow to him whose race is run."
"To heaven thou are fled, and left the nation in tears."
"Can barbarism further go?"

While the procession was steadily escorting the remains back to the depot of the Hudson River Railroad, on 30th Street a group had assembled at the Union Square to pay tribute. Among those offering words of consolation was the Honorable George Bancroft.

Bancroft's oration included the following:

"Our grief at the crime which clothed the continent in mourning, finds no adequate expression in words, no relief in tears. Neither the office with which Mr. Lincoln was invested by the approved choice of a mighty people, nor the most simple-hearted kindness of his nature, could save him from the fiendish passions of the relentless rebellion.

"Waiting millions attend his remains as they are borne in solemn procession over our great rivers, beyond mountains, across prairies, to their final resting place in the valley of the Mississippi. The echoes of his funeral knell will vibrate through the world, and friends of freedom, of very tongue and in every clime, are his mourners."

But in the midst of it all, racial prejudice still sneered at some.

There are strong indications in the very early book *Abraham Lincoln: His Life, Public Services, Death, and Great Funeral Cortege* by John Carroll Power:

"I have said that all party lines were, for the time, hidden from view, but it devolves upon me to notice one exception. Notwithstanding the blending of so many hearts in the great national sorrow, the city authorities of New York, true to their Tammany instincts, took measures to prevent colored people from joining the procession."

Details of the incident have varied somewhat, however the Power account seems very specific:

"They had deferred a procession of their own, on the Wednesday before, in order that 5,000 of their number might be ready to show their love and respect for the emancipator of their race, by joining the procession to escort his remains on their way to the tomb.

"When it was known that the city authorities were trying to keep them out of the procession, Secretary Edwin Stanton interfered, and the order was set aside, but it was too late to give them such assurance of protection as to bring out their full numbers."

However, the president of the Board of Police Commissioners, Thomas C. Acton, apparently stepped into the situation. It was Acton who just a few months earlier enforced "the right of the colored people to ride in the street cars." But of the 5,000 African-Americans who initially planned to be part of the procession event, only between 200 and 300 "could be induced to risk the doubt and uncertainty occasioned by the action of the city authorities."

Those particular citizens were placed "as an appendage" to the Eighth Division, "and to be sure that their rights were respected, Commissioner Acton sent a body of 56 policemen, under Sergeant David Gay, who marched before and behind them in such a way as to be ready in a moment to quell any attempt at violence."

Within the group of a few hundred was a banner prepared by the ladies of the Henry Ward Beecher Church. It was inscribed on one side, "Abraham Lincoln, our Emancipator." On the other side it read, "To Millions of Bondmen, he Liberty Gave."

According to Power, the banner was being carried by four freedmen, meaning those who had been directly freed from slavery. The freedmen, he said, were astonished to learn there were so many more Yankees than "colored" people in the North.

Overall the funeral cortege had remained in New York City a total of around 30 hours. Most of that time, around 22 hours, the corpse of President Lincoln was exposed to public view. During those hours, while estimates varied, it is likely that at least 120,000 persons looked upon those presidential remains.

A conservative estimate at the time (or shortly afterwards) was about 60,000 people were actually part of the New York City funeral procession. Other estimates were higher, but none were anything more scientific than skillful estimations.

Some newspapers at the time put the number of spectators of the procession as it moved to City Hall and then back again to the edge of the Hudson River at 750,000. It may well have been higher.

One correspondent summed it up:

"The more I think of the subject, the more I am impressed with the inadequacy of language to convey a correct idea of the intensity of feeling and the magnitude of the demonstration; but taken in all its bearings, New York City paid a tribute of respect to the memory of Abraham Lincoln, the like of which was never approached in this country before, and has probably not been excelled in the obsequies of any ruler in the history of the world."

All heady observations aside, the boats were ready for another river departure.

"All things being in readiness, the funeral train left the 30th Street Depot at 4:15 p.m. on April 25, leaving an immense multitude of spectators, the men with uncovered heads," wrote one observer. "They then dispersed, to treasure up the memories of that day to the end of their lives."

The next full and official unloading stop for the Lincoln Funeral Train would be Albany, New York.

There were two locomotive engines set apart by the Hudson River Railway Company to lead the Lincoln Funeral Train from New York City to Albany. Both, according to one report, "were most beautifully and appropriately decorated with mourning symbols for the occasion."

Going ahead first was the pilot or escort engine, named The Constitution. Pulling the train the train directly was the engine, The Union, and the "decorations bestowed upon The Union were of the most elaborate and tasteful description."

Coincidentally, it had been The Union that had conveyed the President-elect from Albany to New York, while making a triumphal inaugural trip from Springfield to Washington in 1861.

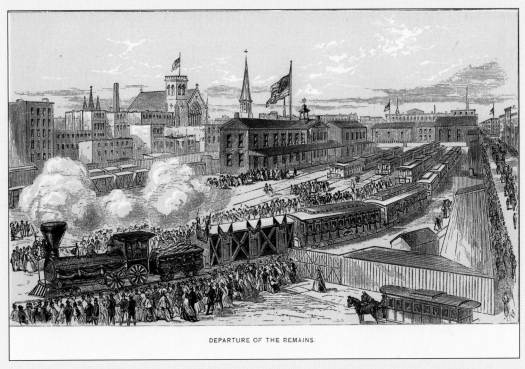

DEPARTURE OF THE REMAINS.

Majestic departure of the remains of President Abraham Lincoln at the train station in New York City on Tuesday afternoon, April 25, 1865. Last of a series of eight drawings at the scene by William Waud. (Author's collection).

The Lincoln Funeral Train moved off into the New York countryside with a strange, almost eerie sound.

"It happened that the usual hoarse clangor of the engine bell was deadened by the tongue being muffled," said one observer, "and as the train moved off it gave an indescribable air of mournfulness and woe to the scene."

At Hastings, the home of naval war hero Commodore David Farragut, the townsfolk were prepared. They had constructed a memorial near the depot that consisted of a four-columned arch draped with mourning flags.

It bore the following inscription:

"We cherish the memory of Abraham Lincoln by supporting the principles of free government, for which he suffered martyrdom."

People of that community were also proud of Farragut, who had been promoted to Vice Admiral just a few months earlier by President Lincoln. Farragut won acclaim for his many naval victories during the Civil War. He might have been most famous for his declaration, "Damn the torpedoes, full speed ahead," during the Battle of Mobile Bay.

At one point among the towns and villages as the train moved along there were 100 school girls, dressed in white, standing along the tracks. At another site the track was arched with a huge memorial with an inscription reading, "The Nation mourns a Nation's loss."

Still further down the track a young lady dressed as the Goddess of Liberty knelt upon a dais. As the train slowly passed one of her hands clasp a flag whose folds were clad in black. Her other hand rested upon a floral anchor. Before her, on the same dais, was a small monument, darkly clad, which was inscribed simply, "Abraham Lincoln."

The crowd was estimated at 7,000 along the tracks and depot at Irvington. Draped banners were everywhere in view at the small village. Next, at Tarrytown, the train passed under an arch of American flags. Nearby were a group of young women dressed in white gowns standing beneath a dome of black velvet and flowers.

Next stop was Ossining, the site of Sing Sing Prison. Again the train passed beneath a large memorial arch. The arch included American flags and 36 individual stars designating each state in the then existing Union. The train stopped briefly there to take on water, and according to a newspaper report, an official of the prison was allowed to board the train and briefly view the body of Lincoln.

Sing Sing had opened as a model prison in the 1820s and became known for its enforcement of absolute silence among prisoners. Those who disobeyed were severely whipped or similarly punished. Early in the 21st century the original cell block for the prison would be turned into a museum.

The memorial arch for the Lincoln Funeral Train on April 25, 1865 at Sing Sing Prison outside of Ossining, New York. *Prints and Photographs Division, Library of Congress.*

At Peekskill, the train again halted for a few minutes.

Just over four years earlier, in 1861, Lincoln had spoken briefly on the train platform at Peekskill. On this funeral trip there was a large picture of President Lincoln near the depot. The picture was surrounded by roses and further decorated with red, white, and blue tassels.

At 6:20 p.m., the Lincoln Funeral Train rolled into Garrison's Landing, just across from the West Point Military Academy and was connected by way of ferry boat. At West Point, a company of regular soldiers and all of the West Point cadets were drawn up in a single line. The cadets, about 1,000 of them, stood in full uniforms with rifles at present arms formation.

While the train was still halted, according to one account, "the cadets all passed through the funeral car and saluted the remains of their late Commander-in-Chief. Meanwhile, salutes were being fired from the west side of the river by the guns at West Point."

As the train pulled away the guns continued to fire and music from the Academy bands could be heard in the distance. In the early darkness torches were blazing and held high by various groups. From jutting rocks came an accompanying chorus of bonfires.

At Cold Spring, under a large arch, a woman in full Goddess of Liberty costume kneeled as the train appeared; at her side were boys, one dressed as a soldier and one dressed as a sailor. Both also kneeled in unison.

The depot at Fishkill was "artistically draped in mourning" and amidst the evergreen finery was, "In God We Trust." Observers said the large crowd at Fishkill occurred because of its attraction to others from surrounding towns and villages. Across the river from Fishkill, at Newburg, a flag "draped in mourning" was displayed from the house where General George Washington was said to have headquartered during the Revolutionary War.

Poughkeepsie was waiting with "a bounteous supper for the entire escort" when the train arrived. Soon after the train stopped, a committee of seven ladies placed a wreath of roses on the coffin of President Lincoln. Outside a cornet band composed of students from the Eastman National Business College provided fanfare.

Guns were firing at Poughkeepsie and children were waving miniature flags in the vast crowd. There was also a delegation from the city government of Albany, along with about 1,200 pupils and Professor Eastman from the National Business College.

"After a stay of nearly one hour, the train moved on," according to one account, "and from this time it was lighted by bonfires and torches, at different stations."

Still another observer offered that this particular phase of the journey, starting at Poughkeepsie and moving westward, "along the entire route the respect and sorrow of the people was appropriately manifested."

Downtown Albany, New York decorated with mourning for the arrival of the Lincoln Funeral Train in April of 1865. *Prints and Photographs Division, Library of Congress.*

Not surprisingly, in the darkness at 8:35 p.m. Rhinebeck, "A torchlight procession enabled the assembled crowds of people to view the imposing funeral cortege as it flitted by."

A report from Hudson at 9:45 p.m. briefly noted, "Thousands of people were assembled, minute guns fired, buildings illuminated and draped in mourning." It added: "Stockport, Stuyvesant and Castleton were passed, at all of which were bonfires or torch lights."

Around 10:55 p.m. that evening, the Lincoln Funeral Train arrived at East Albany. It was dark, dreary, and chilly, but the crowd turned out just the same.

One correspondent wrote this diary-like comment:

"Arrived to find the depot in mourning, bells tolling, cannons firing, soldiers marching, and three companies of firemen bearing torches to light the funeral party across the river to Albany.

"The remains were taken from the car and placed in a hearse. The entire party passed over on ferry boat, and were escorted by a midnight torchlight procession to the State Capitol."

The remains, drawn by four plumed and draped gray horses, was met by various city officials, members of the state legislature, and other distinguished citizens.

Shortly after midnight, the weather that particular April was described as "murky, dry, starlight, still and pleasant."

About a dozen fire companies were assembled there with their "lamp torches," along with three companies of militia from the 10th Regiment, and one company from the 25th Regiment.

"The streets were thronged as they had never been before," observed one account. "A profusion of sable drapery prevailed at the depot, on the boat, and at every point along the route, from the landing at Albany to the platform where the remains lay in state in the Assembly Chamber."

"The smoke and glare of the torch lights, the silent tramp of feet, and the perfect hush of the people, as the cortege moved on its way through the capital of the State, was very impressive," added the observer.

At one o'clock in the very early morning of April 26, the coffin of President Lincoln was once again opened to a group of mourners who had never before seen the lifeless face of the man who lay there.

By morning visitors could see that the whole city was draped in mourning, "with mottoes and inscriptions tastefully displayed at appropriate points."

At the Assembly Chamber itself, the number of people standing to view the body of the President had become massive. The line of those waiting for admission in the morning's dawn was more than a mile in length.

"The crowd, one half of them being ladies, was all pressing towards the portals of the stately edifice," said one report. "The (rail) cars and steamboats arriving that morning brought additional thousands to the city. Adding further that, "many of them were coming from one to two hundred miles away."

Like so many other previous places the coffin itself and the area immediately surrounding it were constantly deluged with fresh flowers. Just as fast as one group of exceptional flowers appeared to be waning, they were removed, and just as many—if not more—were put in their place.

Meanwhile:

"Solemn dirges were performed at intervals by the musical societies and bands. The steam of people continued to pour through the edifice, to take a last look at the distinguished dead, and yet, when the hour arrived for replacing the cover, thousands were still in line pressing their way toward the State House," noted one witness.

Observers at the scene in Albany estimated at one point that people were filing through the Assembly Chamber at the rate of more than four thousand an hour.

Such a turnout, and those that had previously occurred along the journey had a startling effect on the traveling Illinois delegation now visiting in Albany.

"From the time the funeral party started, they had been astonished to witness the immense throngs of people who, night and day, through sunshine and storm, met them at every point to see the great funeral cortege and view the remains," according to an accompanying journalist. "They feared the people of Springfield would be overwhelmed with numbers before they realized the intensity of feeling on the part of people."

There at Albany the Illinois delegation held a hurried consultation and decided it was best for one of their members to go at once to Springfield and to then impress upon the citizens the importance of exerting themselves to the utmost in making suitable preparations for the final ceremonies.

In other words, Springfield must prepare for a swarm of mourning visitors.

At 2 p.m. the coffin was closed and slowly conveyed to a magnificent hearse drawn by eight white horses. It was then escorted by a vast procession, composed of all the military of both Albany and Troy, the fire department, the State and city authorities, about 30 civic associations and citizens generally, to the New York Central Depot, where it was placed on board the hearse car.

Earlier the hearse railroad car and the railroad car that held the Honor Guard "were run up the river five miles to Troy, where they were then taken across the Hudson River on the railroad bridge, and run down the west side to the New York Central Depot, at Albany."

Finally, the train was fully intact and ready to proceed further in its journey. Summarized one correspondent of the departure:

"Never before were such multitudes of people gathered at the Capital of the State (Albany). Everyone seemed fully to realize the solemnity of the occasion. It was estimated that at least 50,000 men, women, and children visited the remains during the twelve and a half hours they were exposed to view. The Central railroad furnished seven of its finest cars, making the same number the train had been composed of before, and at 4 p.m. on Wednesday, April 16, the great funeral cortege resumed its journey westward through the Empire State."

The next "slowdown" stop would be Schenectady, New York.

When the train arrived at Schenectady around 4:45 p.m. there was a surprising multitude of people assembled. The depot, businesses, and dwelling houses everywhere were draped in mourning.

"The women were much affected, many of them crying audibly, and tears coursed down many manly cheeks," noted one present. "The mechanics of the railroad shops all stood in line, with heads uncovered, and the utmost silence prevailed."

Off to the side of the Schenectady depot, signal men stood quietly as well, holding white square signal flags bordered with black.

At tiny Amsterdam the Lincoln Funeral Train neared the depot at 5:25 p.m. One aboard reasoned that the crowd awaiting them at the depot, was evidently from the country, as it was but a small village, and the line (of people) was a mile long."

Not out of the ordinary however, "The train passed through an arch, decorated with red, white, and blue, and draped mourning. The village bells tolled from the time the train arrived, and continued until we passed out of hearing."

It was 5:45 p.m. when the train reached the hamlet of Fonda.

"Depot, houses, and an arch across the railroad—all decorated with flags and draped in mourning," went one brief narrative of the encounter there. "Minute guns were fired as the train arrived, and continued until it passed out of hearing."

The train's route took it along the valley of the Mohawk River to a point where the rail tracks actually ran under the picturesque Palatine Bridge. The time was 6:25 p.m. The bridge had been artistically decorated with flags intertwined with mourning emblems. As the train approached, there was a white cross erected on a grassy mound not far from the track. The cross itself, robed in evergreens and mourning drape, bore this inscription:

"We have prayed for you; now we can only weep."

It had been prearranged that the Lincoln Funeral Train would make a full stop at St. Johnsville. Planners had realized the passengers would eventually need a rest stop on the long journey—refreshments too.

"When the train arrived at St. Johnsville, a bounteous supper was waiting," noted a passenger, "and the depot was elaborately draped in mourning."

Furthermore, there were 24 young ladies "from the most wealthy and refined families of the village and surrounding country, dressed in white with black velvet badges, waiting on tables. After supper, these young ladies assembled, entered the hearse car, and placed a wreath of flowers on the coffin, and then the train moved on in its westward course."

Postcard depicts painting of Abraham Lincoln by William E. Marshall, 1864. The painting was then property of The New-York Historical Society.

Those aboard the train at this point settled in for generally a long period of nightfall ahead.

"It was now quite dark," indicated one passenger regarding the departure into the night from St. Johnsville, "and the remaining distance to Buffalo occupied the whole time until daylight."

Among the passengers the general consensus thus far in the long journey from Washington to Springfield was fairly positive. "Overall the passengers were pleasantly surprised, despite the grim task of it all," noted an observer as the train moved along somewhere between St. Johnsville and Little Falls. "The response was far greater than anyone anticipated."

Later one correspondent would state the case with the funeral train more or less at the halfway mark in a most unique journey in a similar accord:

"Those on board the train remember this as having been the most remarkable portion of the whole route for its continuous and hearty demonstrations of respect—if any part could be so designated, where all were without precedent.

"Bonfires and torch lights illumined the road the entire distance. Minute guns were fired at so many points that it seemed almost continuous. Singing societies and bands of music were so numerous that after passing a station the sound of a dirge or requiem would scarcely die away in the distance, until it would be caught up at the town or village they were approaching.

"Thus through the long hours of the night did the funeral cortege received such honors that it seemed more like the march of a mighty conqueror than respect to the remains of one of the most humble sons of earth."

At 7:35 p.m. the train slowed to a halt in Little Falls, New York. Almost immediately a group of women were allowed to board and bring a wreath of flowers in the form of a shield and a cross to the coffin.

It bore the following inscription:

"The ladies of Little Falls, through their committee, present these flowers. The shield, as an emblem of the protection which our beloved President has ever proved to the liberties of the American people. The cross, of his ever faithful trust in God, and the wreath as a token that we mingle our tears with those of our afflicted nation."

The flowered piece was signed by Mrs. S.M. Richmond, Mrs. E. W. Hopkins, Mrs. Powers Green, Mrs. J. H. Bucklin, Miss Minnie Hill, Miss Helen Brooks, Miss Maria Brooks, and Miss Marry Shaw.

As the flowers were being placed into the coffin, still another band stood outside performing a hymn. As a result, "Women and men were moved to tears at this exhibition of heartfelt regard," noted one who was present.

There was a group of 36 ladies waiting at the depot in Herkimer when the train rolled by at 7:50 p.m. The women wore white dresses with black sashes and held American flags representing the 36 states of the Union. Typically a local band was playing soulful music.

Document signed by President Abraham Lincoln and countersigned by Edwin Stanton authorizing the appointment of Wm. G. Laverty as First Lieutenant in the Veteran Reserve Corps, with seal intact. Approximately 19 and one half inches by 16 inches, unframed. *Skinner, Inc.*, estimated at $3,000–$3,500.

Since the train did not stop but only slowed for Herkimer, mourners had to throw wreaths of flowers on board as the train barely moved down the tracks.

At the Ilion station the Remington gun factory was brilliantly illuminated in the distance. There was a torch light procession as the train moved by, and there were young boys dressed in Zouave uniforms. The costumes represented outfits worn by French army Zouaves who had originally been natives of Algeria and Morocco. Later the uniforms were worn by some units of native Frenchmen during the Civil War.

The torch light was described as "gorgeous" as the train glided through Utica around 8:25 p.m. that evening. A large crowd of people had gathered around the tracks with a multitude of banners. The depot and other Utica buildings were fully draped in mourning.

Just ahead, "as the train swept by Whitesboro and Oriskany, the people were gathered in crowds around large bonfires, waving flags trimmed with mourning," wrote one observer.

Fittingly, "it was raining heavily when the train arrived at Rome (New York), but there was an immense crowd assembled at the depot, which was richly draped in mourning," said one narrative. "A band of music on the platform was playing a death march."

There was a company of firemen lined up holding burning torches when the train arrived around 9:50 p.m. at Oneida. A prominent arch over the track bore the inscription, "We mourn with the Nation." Again there was a significant crowd despite the darkness and the weather.

Just a short distance down the track, a passenger would note burning torches and blazing bonfires at Casnastoa, Canaserga, Chittenango, Kirkville, and Manius—all in a similar but dramatic manner.

Shortly after 11 p.m. the Lincoln Funeral Train pulled into the depot at Syracuse, and according to one passenger, "the scene was grand and imposing." The depot and adjoining buildings were "almost covered with insignia of sorrow. Many dwellings were illuminated and mourning drapery was suspended around the windows. Tears coursed down the cheeks of both men and women."

It was also at Syracuse that a flower and a note were handed to officials onboard. The note read, "The last tribute of respect from Mary Virginia Raynor, a little girl of three years of age." It was dated April 26, 1865. The child's note was laid on the President's coffin by one of the generals in attendance.

A small notation was made by one lingering witness regarding the train's passage through the town of Palmyra about 2:15 a.m. on the morning of April 27. It said briefly:

"The (Palmyra) depot is nicely decorated, and men, women, and children flock about the hearse car."

More than an hour later the train rumbled into Rochester. The military was well represented on the north side of the railroad station. Soldiers lined up to pay respect included the 54th National Guard State Troops, first company of Veteran Reserves, hospital-bound soldiers, a battery attached to the 25th Brigade, and the first company of what was then called the Union Blues. The Independent and New Marine regimental band played an impressive arrangement of funeral-related selections.

Meanwhile, on the south side of the station were the mayor of Rochester, city council members, other dignitaries, military officials, and General John Williams. Additionally, there were thousands of ordinary citizens who had gathered locally and from many other locations.

After Crofts, Corfu, Alden, Wende, and Lancaster, the funeral train moved into the dark countryside of New York State. "Soon after daylight," one correspondent recorded, "in passing a farm house, a group of children were seen waving towards the train with flags trimmed in mourning."

At 7 a.m. the Lincoln Funeral Train reached Buffalo, New York.

There was the immediate noise of tolling bells and the firing of cannon throughout the community. Moreover, the train, according to one report, "was met at the depot by a large concourse of people."

Just after the president's assassination this editorial had appeared addressed to the people in the *Buffalo Daily Express*:

"How reverently Abraham Lincoln was loved by the common people; how much they leaned upon the strength of his heroic character, in the great trial through which he led them; how perfect a trust they reposed in his wisdom, his integrity, his patriotism, and the fortitude of his faithful heart; how great a sphere he filled in the constitution of their hopes, they did not know before.

"The shock of consternation, grief, and horror, which revealed it to them, was then

The funeral procession for President Abraham Lincoln as it goes through Buffalo, New York in April 1865. *Prints and Photographs Division, Library of Congress.*

Secretary of State (William) Hunter. Because of this, there were no formal preparations made for the arrival of the funeral train itself; however, the train was indeed met with what was already described at the scene as "a large concourse" of people.

Citizens there, headed by the military, formed an "impromptu procession" and the coffin was taken to a fine hearse, "which was covered with white satin and silver lace. The coffin was elevated so as to be seen at a long distance."

The procession moved ever so slowly along the principal streets of Buffalo, with the distant sounds of funeral music provided by a local band. The procession reached St. James Hall about 9:30 a.m. There the body, in the presence of the accompanying Guard of Honor and Union Continentals, was placed on a dais in the great Hall.

As the remains were carried into the Hall, the Buffalo St. Cecelia Society sang, "with much feeling," the song "Rest, Spirit, Rest," after which the Society placed an "elegantly formed" harp, made of choice white flowers, at the head of the coffin. According to witnesses, "the coffin was overshadowed by a crepe canopy, and the space lighted up by a large chandelier in the ceiling."

Probably the most distinguished mourner there in Buffalo to view the remains of President Lincoln was former President Millard Fillmore.

Fillmore, the 13th president of the United States, was the last official member of the Whig Party to hold the office of President. Although both Lincoln and Fillmore had been members of the Whig Party at one time,

undoubtedly the most profound that ever fell upon a people.

"The strong men of the nation wept together like children. Never, do we believe, was there exhibited such a spectacle of many tears, wrung from stout hearts, by bitter anguish, as in the streets of every city, town, and hamlet in these United States, on Saturday last.

"Ah, there is and was a deep planting of love for Abraham Lincoln in the hearts of his countrymen! Noble soul, honest heart, wise statesman, upright magistrate, brave old patriot, the nation was orphaned by thy death and felt the grief of orphanage."

The city of Buffalo had consequently held a major observance of Lincoln's funeral on April 19, as the nation had been urged to do by leaders in Washington including acting during the Civil War the former president had generally opposed Lincoln. However, after Lincoln's death, Fillmore was oddly somewhat supportive of the Reconstruction under President Andrew Johnson.

At time of the funeral train's arrival, Fillmore lived in a fine home within the confines of Buffalo, and was one of the community's most highly regarded citizens.

It was estimated that 40,000 to 50,000 persons viewed the remains of Lincoln at Buffalo. In addition to Americans it was reported that a large number of Canadians came to Buffalo during that day, "to manifest their sympathy by taking part in the procession and viewing the remains."

The funeral party aboard the train itself was hosted as guests of the city, and were quartered in the then highly regarded Mansion House. Meanwhile, all trade and business about the city was suspended out of respect for the occasion.

At 8 p.m. the coffin was closed at St. James Hall. Around 9 p.m. it was carefully transported back to the railway depot. Around 10 p.m. it departed in the darkness, heading even further westward.

Shortly after midnight on Friday, April 28, the funeral train arrived at the station in Dunkirk.

One account of that stop was as follows:

"The principle feature of the scene was a group of 36 young ladies, representing the States of the Union, dressed in white with black scarves on their shoulders. All were kneeling and each held a national flag.

"It was a beautiful tableau, as seen at the midnight hours by the glare of more than a hundred lamps and torches.

"When the train stopped, the young ladies entered the funeral car and placed a wreath of flowers and evergreens on the coffin. The firing of guns, tolling of bells, and the band performing a requiem, combined

The Lincoln Funeral Train as it prepares to leave Buffalo, New York, in April of 1865.
Prints and Photographs Division, Library of Congress.

with the other parts to present a spectacle such as never before been witnessed on the shores of Lake Erie."

The next stop for the train was Westfield. It was about 1 a.m. in the early morning.

At Westfield the crew took on wood and water while a group of five ladies placed a cross and a wreath of roses on the coffin of President Lincoln. One of the women was Mrs. Lillian Drake, the wife of a Union colonel who had been killed in battle at Cold Harbor. Another woman was identified as Miss Elizabeth Tucker.

The inscription on the wreath read:
"Ours the Cross, Thine, the Crown."

An observer at Westfield concluded of the scene and the women, "All of them were affected to tears, and considered it a sacred privilege to kiss the coffin."

Then it was on to the New York and Pennsylvania state line, where "a bonfire was blazing, flags were draped, and a larger number of people were assembled."

On board the funeral train Major General Dix took leave of the official procession, and a number of civic officials from both Pennsylvania and Ohio came aboard.

This was the schedule for New York:

(MONDAY, APRIL 24, 1865)
New York City arrive 10:50 a.m.

(TUESDAY, APRIL 25)
New York City depart 4:15 p.m.
Fort Washington
Yorkville
Mount St. Vincent
Manhattanville
Harlem
Spuyten Duyvel Creek
Yonkers
Hastings
Dobbs Ferry
Irvington
Tarrytown
Sing Sing (Osining)
Oscawana Crugers
Peekskill

Garrison's Landing (West Point) arrive 6:20 p.m.
Cold Spring (Duchess Junction)
Fishkill-on-the-Hudson arrive 6:55 p.m.
North Hamburg
Poughkeepsie arrive 7:10 p.m.
Hyde Park
Staatsburg
Rhinebeck arrive 8:35 p.m.
Barrytown
Tivoli
Germantown
Catskill
Hudson arrive 9:45 p.m.
Stockport
Stuyvesant
Schodack
Castleton
Greenbrush / East Albany arrive 10:55 p.m.
Rail Factory
Troy
Cohoes
West Troy
Albany

(WEDNESDAY, APRIL 26)
Albany depart 4 p.m.
Schenectady
Crainesville
Hoffman's
Canajoharie
Amsterdam arrive 5:25 p.m.
Akin
Fonda arrive 5:45 p.m.
Yost
Sprakers
East Creek
Palatine Bridge arrive 6:25 p.m.
Fort Plain arrive 6:32 p.m.
St. Johnsville arrive 6:47 p.m.
Little Falls arrive 7:35 p.m.
Herkimer arrive 7:50 p.m.
Ilion arrive 7:56 p.m.
Frankfort
Utica arrive 8:25 p.m.
Whitesboro
Oriskany

Rome arrive 9:10 p.m.
Green's Corners
Verona
Oneida arrive 9:50 p.m.
Wampsville
Canastota
Canaserga
Chittenango
Kirkville
Manlius
Syracuse arrive 11:30 p.m.
Canton
Jordon
North Weedsport
Port Byron
Clyde
Memphis arrive 12 p.m.

(THURSDAY, APRIL 27, 1865)
Lyons
Newark
Palmyra arrive 2:15 a.m.
Meridian
Fairport arrive 2:50 a.m.
Brighton
Rochester arrive 3:20 a.m.
Coldwater
Chili
Churchville
Bergen
West Bergen
Batavia arrive 5:18 a.m.
Crofts
Oakfield
Corfu
Alden
Wende
Town Line
Lancaster
Buffalo arrive 7 a.m. depart 10 p.m.
New Hamburgh (Hamburg)
North Evans
Lake View
18 Mile Creek
Derby
Evans Centre
Saw Mill (Angola)
Farnham

Irving
Silver Creek
Sheridan Station (Lackawanna)

(FRIDAY, APRIL 28, 1865)
Dunkirk arrive 12:10 a.m.
Van Buren
Salem
Brockton
Westfield arrive 1 a.m.
Ripley Crossing
Quincy

The Lincoln Funeral Train once again touched the state of Pennsylvania when it crossed the state line from New York State. At 1:47 a.m. that Friday, it reached North East, Pennsylvania.

It was there that 12-year-old Leonora Crawford carefully climbed aboard the train and presented a cross and wreath with the words, "Rest In Peace."

And it was also there that the mayor of Erie, F. F. Farrar, came aboard the funeral train. Accompanying the mayor to the next stop at Erie were George W. Starr, F.B. Vincent, E. P. Bennett, J.T. Walsher, and Captain F. A. Roe of the United States Navy.

The train arrived in Erie around 2:50 a.m. with those aboard apparently exhausted from the long day and night's journey. It prompted a departure from what had been the standard flow of events even in the dead of night.

This report from a correspondent:

"The citizens of Erie were making arrangements to give suitable reception to the honored remains, when they were informed by the Superintendent of the Cleveland & Erie Railroad that the funeral escort had made a special request that no public demonstration be made at that place (Erie), in order to give them an opportunity to repose.

The request was unauthorized, but it never the less deprived them of a mournful pleasure."

Even so, "notwithstanding this, a large number of people were assembled at the Erie depot, where a transparency was displayed with the inscription:

"Abraham Lincoln may die, but the principles embalmed in his blood will live forever."

Later the train passed through Girard, where one aboard noted:

"A large number of people were collected at the depot, which was draped with mourning and illuminated with bonfires."

Next, at around 2:27 a.m., the train reached Springfield, Pennsylvania. Again there was a substantial assembly of people bearing lighted torches.

Regarding the running of the train from Erie on to Cleveland, Ohio there was every attempt by railway officials to duplicate the earlier journey President Lincoln had made on the same railroad in 1861. The locomotive, the William Case, was the same. The original engineer, William Congden, however was deceased, and the engine was now run by John Benjamin. The fireman in 1861, George Martin, had been promoted to engineer, but had requested the "privilege" of again acting as fireman on the funeral train.

Things were going well.

As one traveler commented of the trip thus far:

"Between Buffalo and Cleveland the people of New York, Pennsylvania and of Ohio, testified in great numbers and with tasteful symbols and elaborate demonstrations, respect which was heartfelt, and sorrow which sought close sympathy.

This was the schedule for western Pennsylvania:

(FRIDAY, APRIL 28, 1865)

North East arrive 1:47 a.m.
Wesleyville (Harbor Creek)
Erie arrive 2:50 a.m.
Mill Creek
Swanville
Fairview
Girard
Springfield

Heartland

(Ohio, Indiana)

Everywhere deep sorrow has been manifested, and the feeling seems, if possible, to deepen, as we move West-ward with the remains to their final resting place.

—*New York Times* reporter writing in
Cleveland, Ohio April 28, 1865.

At this point in the Lincoln Funeral Train's movement, a few trends became apparent across the land.

First was the weather.

It was the month of April. It was a time of the year in the East and in the Middle West when the weather was chilly and rainy. In fact, the train traveled the entire route much of the time, day and night, in varying rain—from light mist to virtual downpours. A century later, one popular song would call such weather "April showers," but they were also just as well known as part of the spring season in the 19th century too.

Second were the surging crowds.

From the beginning, the military crowds and the others foresaw large crowds—in fact immense turnouts—in the larger cities that had been included in the train's meandering schedule. What hardly anyone expected were the throngs of people lining the relatively isolated tracks along the route, or the additional throngs surrounding the depots of obscure little towns and villages. Time and again correspondents or other witness passengers were deeply impressed by the sight of great numbers of people who had no doubt journeyed significant distances by primitive means—horseback, wagon, or buggy—in the most rural and rugged regions of that part of the country.

Thus, at every point, people were doggedly destined to brave elements for such an historic and unprecedented event. "History does not record a more touching spectacle than the passing of this funeral train through the most populous states of the Union," read a statement issued decades afterward by a firm in Toledo, Ohio. Along with the statement was a black and white photograph of the Lincoln Funeral Train itself. It was released by the Lamson Brothers Company—a legendary department store— after all those years because, "now that a united nation reveres the memory of Lincoln and everything connected with his life and death, we thought it appropriate that we should present this picture to the brave men to whom our nation is so greatly indebted."

It turns out that Myron H. Lamson, father of the Lamson Brothers Company founders, had enlisted as a mechanic in the Union Army during the Civil War. Eventually, he served as assistant foreman during the construction of the presidential car converted to funeral car.

At 3:47 a.m. on Friday, April 28, the Lincoln Funeral Train arrived at the first station in Ohio. The crowd at Conneaut was large and somber in the light rain. The depot itself was draped in mourning cloths.

The scene was very similar as the train next moved through Kingsville, Ohio.

Guns were already firing in the distance as the train approached Ashtabula, and still another depot was draped in mourning. Observers also recorded a large number of American flags unfurled in that area. Crowds ignored the darkness to dawn and were standing in reverence in places like Geneva, Madison, Perry, Painesville, and Mentor. The train pulled into Willoughby at 6:08 a.m. and there was this account:

"Notwithstanding the early morning hour, a number of very aged men leaning on their staffs with their snow-white locks uncovered. Hundreds of watchers looked longingly at the sable cortege gliding by."

Major General Joseph Hooker, a prominent Civil War figure who was then commanding the Northern Department of Ohio, joined the funeral party at Wickliffe. It was 6:20 a.m. Hooker, under General Orders No. 72, took command of the entire train. Among the staff now with him Adjutant General B. R. Cowan, Assistant Adjutant General John T. Mercer, Quarter Master General Merrill Barlow, Surgeon General R.N. Barr, Colonel S. D. Maxwell, and private secretary F. A. Marble.

Besides the military boarding at Wickliffe there were a number of prominent citizens from northern Ohio, mostly representing the city of Cleveland. The Cleveland group, which numbered about 25, was reportedly "appointed at Cleveland as a committee to attend the funeral procession from the State Line to that city (Cleveland)."

At the very next stop, at Euclid around 6:32 a.m., additional numbers of Cleveland citizens boarded the train and joined the earlier Cleveland escort committee.

Nashville, the Lincoln Train engine, prepared to pull the train in Cleveland, Ohio. *Prints and Photographs Division, Library of Congress.*

A magnificent arch immediately attracted attention among the passengers as the train actually pulled into the city of Cleveland around 7 a.m. Friday morning. In huge letters the arch bore the simple inscription: "Abraham Lincoln."

Directly under the arch was a female regaled in costume that was representing the Goddess of Liberty. The costumed woman proudly held an American flag. Both the flag and her Liberty cap were braided in mourning. A hard-driving rain did not dampen spirits in Cleveland. "An immense multitude thronged the streets," according to one report, "and as the train arrived a national salute of thirty-six guns was fired." The firings continued every half-hour until sunset.

The people of Cleveland were prepared because they had planned ahead. As soon as it was definitely determined that the remains of President Lincoln would pass through Cleveland on their way to Springfield, "measures were taken to extend to them the honor due from a grateful people to their beloved Chief Magistrate."

At a meeting back on April 19, city council member Amos Townsend had introduced a resolution to appoint a committee to make the necessary preparations. The committee included Mayor George B. Sentee, council president Thomas Jones Jr., Joseph Sturges, Ansel Roberts, and Townsend. Appropriately, the meeting was held on the same day more or less designated as one for national mourning.

On the very next day, April 20, the Cleveland Board of Trade also formed a committee that included community leaders such as Philo Chamberlin, R.T. Lyon, J.R. Freeman, S. F. Lester, W. Murray, and A.J. Begges. The purpose of the civic committee was "to co-operate with the committee from the City Council on matters pertaining to the reception of the remains of the President."

By the Thursday before Friday's arrival of the funeral train, the pace at Cleveland was hectic.

"Every train that arrived on the railroads during Thursday and on Thursday night was filled," according to one narrative, "and all the hotels were crowded, and hundreds of persons were unable to procure even a sleeping place upon the floor (of the hotels)."

Around the city that Thursday before the train arrived, "the symbols of mourning were universal. Men, women, and children, of all classes and conditions, wore some badge or symbol of sorrow." Already by Thursday evening citizens on Superior, Euclid, Prospect, and around the Square were busily decorating houses and businesses with mourning cloth. "Along the line designated for the passing of the procession," said one account, "the draping was very elaborate, tasteful, and almost universal."

Meanwhile, a final order for the day was issued by Colonel James Barnett, Chief Marshal. It read in part:

"The following program of arrangements is announced for the solemnization of the obsequies of Abraham Lincoln, late President of the United States, in this city, on Friday, April 28th.

"The bells of the city will be tolled during the moving of the procession. The shipping in the harbor, and the proprietors of public houses and others, are requested to display their colors at half-mast during the day. It is earnestly requested that all places of business or amusement be closed during the day. Vehicles of all kinds will be withdrawn from the streets through which the procession will pass, and none will be allowed in the procession except those designated. Delegations will be promptly at their places of rendezvous, prepared to march at the appointed time."

By the time the funeral train arrived at the depot the anxious citizens of Cleveland were ready.

The waiting funeral procession alone was immense and impressive. Military and Civil associations had formed at the Euclid Street station for nearly as far as the eye could see. It extended to include a full six divisions, each headed by its own band. When the train stopped, the casket was almost immediately

Funeral procession for President Abraham Lincoln as it unfolded in Cleveland, Ohio. *Prints and Photographs Division, Library of Congress.*

loaded onto a "magnificent" hearse, "draped with a huge American flag trimmed with mourning."

In a way the procession moved with stunning precision. As it was described in one account: "The long perspective of Euclid Street stretched away in unrivaled beauty, and the procession, with its solid column, great length, and imposing display, made up a scene never equaled in Cleveland. There was scarcely any variation from the published order of the Chief Marshal in the formation of the procession."

First in the procession came the Military Escort, led by the Camp Chase Band. The escort consisted of the 29th Regiment Ohio National Guard and the Eighth Independent Battery. The Escort was followed by Major General Hooker, staff, and officers of the Army on horseback.

Lincoln funeral hearse pulled in Cleveland, Ohio, by a team of white horses in April 1865. *Prints and Photographs Division, Library of Congress.*

As previously mentioned, General Hooker was considered a major figure of the Civil War, and so here on the streets of Cleveland he was a near-legend. Following the Battle of Fredericksburg, he was given command of the Army of the Potomac. After a less-than-sterling performance at Chancellorsville, President Lincoln relieved him of command. Later Hooker led forces from the Army of the Potomac at the Battle of Lookout Mountain.

Eventually, the general, sometimes known as "Fighting Joe," was given considerable reign by Secretary of War Stanton regarding the Lincoln Funeral Train. As the train traveled through Ohio, Hooker was mainly in command. Right after General Hooker in the procession was the Ohio Governor Brough and staff, and the pall bearers, all in carriages. The hearse was next, followed by the Escort of Honor, which had accompanied the remains since they left Washington. Following that were various committees, the civic guard of honor, and the clergy. The first division had been under the direction of the Colonel O. H. Payne, assistant marshal.

The second division, under the direction of councilman Amos Townsend, was led by the Detroit City Band. The city of Detroit had brought a delegation of about 500 by train earlier. Besides the Detroit City Band, they also brought the Light Guard Band.

There was also a delegation of about 200 people from Meadville in the second division. Each member of the delegation wore a larger badge upon the lapel of their coat with the single word, "Meadville."

On and on the divisions marched.

The sixth division included the likes of the German Benevolent Mutual Society, Lodge 14 of the Colored Masons, The Colored Equal Rights League, Sons of Temperance, and finally the Seamen's Union "carrying a small full-rigged bark (sailing ship with multiple masts), with a flag at half-mast."

The remarkable procession moved through Euclid Street to Erie Street, down Erie to Superior Street, from there to what was described by one correspondent as a "beautiful temple" in a public park known as the Square. According to one report: "The procession had moved slowly and solemnly, without stop or detention, until it reached the Square. As it neared the western end of Euclid Street, the number of people began to increase until the sidewalks and far into the street became a solid mass; but there was no noise or confusion in the crowd that lined the streets on the line of march."

Now they were stopped before the "temple" with its pagoda-style roof. The structure was 24 feet by 36 feet and stood "to the cornice," about 14 feet tall. Inside was what was described as a "gorgeous" catafalque. The President's coffin was carefully laid on a dais, about two feet above the floor of the catafalque.

The columns of the platform were wreathed with evergreens and white flowers, and trimmed with mourning cloth. Meanwhile, black cloth fringed with silver was draped from the corners and the center of the overhanging canopy, and they were looped back to the standing columns.

The floor and sides of the dais were also covered with black cloth, gathered in folds, and further decorated with black and white crepe. In the center of the canopy was a large star of black velvet, ornamented with 36 silver stars representing the States of the Union.

More extensively the dais was covered with flowers, and a figure representing the Goddess of Liberty had been placed at the head of the coffin. Above the ceiling this pagoda temple was hung with festoons of evergreens and flowers. Lamps were attached to the pillars of the catafalque, and also attached to the columns of the temple, providing a distinguished light throughout the day and night.

To mourners, it was an awesome sight. "This temple seemed, in daylight, as if it was a creation of fairy land," lavished one correspondent, "and when lighted up with all the lanterns, and standing out amid the surrounding darkness, looked more like the realization of an enchanted castle than the work of men's hands."

Undoubtedly, it must have been a most expensive tribute. "The cost of it must have been very great," observed one journalist candidly, "and I have been thus detailed in the description because there is nothing comparable to it at any other place on the whole journey. This large expenditure on the part of the citizens of Cleveland, to prepare a few hours resting place for the remains of Abraham Lincoln, on their way to the tomb, was only a faint symbol of the sacrifice they had already made, and were still willing to make, in support of the principles for which he was assassinated."

All day in Cleveland guns were being fired in the distance by the Eighth Independent Battery, Ohio National Guard. Also during the afternoon bands from other cities, as well as from Cleveland, were stationed on the balconies of hotels and other prominent buildings. Their mournful music was said to be as constant as the falling rain in the city.

The saloons of Cleveland were all closed during the stay of the funeral party in the city, by proclamation from the Mayor. Further, in other to control the movements of the vast multitude, all the streets leading to the Park were fenced up and gates placed at the center. Military guards in heavy numbers were positioned about the Park and the building structure itself.

At the Square religious services were being conducted by Right Reverend Bishop William McIlvaine of the Protestant Episcopal Church. The Bishop ultimately advanced to the coffin and read from the Burial Service of the Episcopal Church, which began: "I am the resurrection and the life, saith the Lord; him that believeth in me shall though he were dead, yet shall he live; and whosever livith and believeth in me shall never die."

Bishop McIlvaine then offered "an eloquent prayer," in which he prayed that this great affliction may be of good to the people. He prayed for a blessing on Secretary

Seward, whom had been nearly assassinated. For President Andrew Johnson, he asked that he might be led to follow the "great example set him by his illustrious predecessor."

Once the religious services had been concluded, those who had been part of the long and sober procession were allowed to file through the structure and pass by the President's casket.

Invalid soldiers from the military hospital, who had been kept inside the enclosure and away from the heavy rain, were next allowed to move on pass the casket. "And," according to one witness, "many a bronzed veteran's eyes were wet as he gazed upon one who had lain down his life for his country."

After the procession lines and the invalid soldiers, the public was finally admitted and thousands silently and slowly moved in "without haste or confusion." Two columns of spectators, one on of each side of the casket, began filing past the Lincoln coffin at the rate of about 80 persons per minute. At intervals attending ladies covered the coffin and surrounding area with fresh flowers.

The flow of people was from then on steady and almost endless. One estimate was that more than 50,000 had viewed the remains through the day and into the night. None were allowed to pause, all moved in a muffled marching pace.

At ten minutes past 10 p.m. in the evening, the coffin was closed and the crowds were turned away. "Up to the last moment there was a stream of people passing through the building," wrote one observer, "and if the remains had been exposed well after midnight there would undoubtedly have been the same interest manifested to take one last look."

At ten minutes past 11 p.m. in the evening, the coffin was removed from the Pavilion and placed in the waiting hearse. The escort back to the depot would include the 29th Regiment Ohio National Guard, the General Committee of Arrangements, the Military Guard of Honor riding in carriages, the Civic Guard of Honor bearing a flambeaux, or flaming torch, on a long pole used in parade fashion; the Father Mathew Temperance Society; and the Eureka Lodge of Masons.

Promptly the cortege proceeded down Superior Street, where it was led by three bands playing various funeral marches and hymns. After Vineyard Street, the procession ended up near the funeral train, where the casket would once again be ceremoniously put aboard.

While much of these proceedings were unfolding, another grand plan was underway for a future stop of the funeral train.

Elsewhere in the city of Cleveland the editor of the *Chicago Journal*, Charles L. Wilson, was there to observe and serve as chairman of a group then known as the Committee of One Hundred. These were a group of citizens appointed by the City Council of Chicago. Their plans were "to proceed to Michigan City (Indiana) to receive the remains of President Lincoln, escort them to Chicago, and accompany them to Springfield."

Wilson quietly met with members of the escort party there in Cleveland to work out the details of that escort. He also relayed to the funeral train authorities that Lincoln's train would be met in Michigan City by a group of 41 organizations and societies representing 25,000 people. And they would be working directly with the Chief Marshal in Chicago to become part of the overall Chicago procession.

Rain continued to fall into the dark night.

At midnight, the Lincoln Funeral Train slowly departed from Cleveland, heading steadfastly into the heartland of Ohio, which had also now become the heartland of America.

For the record, the pilot engine just ahead of the funeral train on the run from Cleveland to Columbus was named Louisville. It was under the charge of assistant superintendent William Blee and master mechanic W.F. Smith, with E. VanCamp as engineer and C. Van Cam as fireman.

Meanwhile the engine of the funeral train itself was named the Nashville with George

Alternative Lincoln Funeral Train engine, at right, in the Cleveland, Ohio, train station in April of 1865. *Prints and Photographs Division, Library of Congress.*

Ravenna, Ohio, courthouse shown draped with mourning bunting with crowd gathered during the April 1865 funeral rites for President Lincoln. *Prints and Photographs Division, Library of Congress.*

West aboard as engineer and Peter Hugo as fireman. T.J. Higgins, the superintendent of telegraph, also accompanied the train, carrying the necessary telegraph instruments "to be used in case of an accident."

The small towns down the line from Cleveland were constantly impressive.

Noted one report: "Among the towns worthy of special mention, on account of their costly and elaborate demonstrations, were Berea, Olmstead, Columbia, Grafton, LaGrange, Wellington, Rochester, New London, Greenwich, Shiloh, Selby and Crestline, the latter place being reached at seven minutes past 4 a.m."

"Mottoes and inscriptions expressive of the sorrow of the people were everywhere visible," it continued. "Through the rain and darkness they came, bearing lanterns and torches, that they might obtain a passing view of the great funeral pageant."

On Saturday, April 29, at around 5:20 a.m., the train arrived in Cardington. Again mourners stood bareheaded in the rain as the train slowed. There was an immense crowd around the depot. In front of the depot, over the doors and windows, was a large white banner inscribed: "He sleeps in the blessing of the poor, whose fetters God commanded him break."

Like hundreds of other places along the way, the train departed Cardington to the sound of firing guns and tolling bells. Views from the train in the sunrise seemed like so many before them. Ashley, Eden, Delaware, Berlin, Lewis Center, Orange, Westerville, and Worthington "all presented the same appearance of depots draped in mourning, with mottoes, descriptions, and increasing crowds of people."

About five miles before the Columbus station, an elderly woman appeared along the railroad tracks. She was bareheaded and her hair was disheveled. Tears were rolling down her cheeks as she extended her arms toward the passing train. In one hand she held a bouquet of wildflowers, and in the other she clutched a black sable scarf. Some aboard the train raised their hands as a gesture to her mute offering.

At 7:30 a.m. that Saturday morning, the Lincoln Funeral Train arrived in Columbus, Ohio. Despite a heavy downpour the previous night, the rain had ceased by the time the train had pulled into the station. Even the gloomy and overcast skies had broken away briefly, allowing the barest of morning sun to filter through.

It had now been fourteen days since the nation was horrified by the news of President Lincoln's assassination in Washington, D.C. The people of Columbus had been planning almost every minute since then.

Statehouse at Columbus, Ohio, is decorated for the arrival of the Lincoln Funeral Train and for services to be held there for President Abraham Lincoln. *Prints and Photographs Division, Library of Congress.*

Days in advance the Order of Procession had been established in a large public meeting. The following was issued by the Adjutant General's Office there in Columbus.

ORDER OF PROCESSION:

1. The remains of Abraham Lincoln, late President of the United States, will arrive in the city of Columbus, at 7 o'clock a.m. Saturday, the 29th instant, at the Union Depot.

2. The Funeral escort will consist of the 88th Ohio Volunteers Infantry.

3. Officers of the army, not on duty with troops, are respectfully invited to participate in the obsequies. They will report to Major James Van Voost, 218th U.S. Infantry, at Headquarters, Tod Barracks, at 6 o'clock a.m. Saturday.

4. Detachments of the army and volunteer organizations upon duty with the escort, will be assigned positions on application to Capt. L. Nichols, Tod Barracks. They will appear with side arms only, and will report at 6 o'clock a.m. Saturday.

5. All military officers to be in uniform, and with side arm. The usual badge of mourning will be worn on the left arm and sword hilt.

6. In order to prevent confusion at the entrance gate, all who are not in line of the procession will form after the left of the procession has entered Capitol Square in two ranks, on the outside of the Square fence, on High Street, running north to Broad, south to State, hence east to Broad. They will enter the west gate four abreast, in regular order, by inward march of each rank, and in no other way.

Even before that the Adjutant General's Office had issued this official imperative:

"Major John W. Skiles, Eighty-eighth Ohio Volunteers Infantry, is hereby appointed Chief Marshal of ceremonies in honor of the remains of the late President Lincoln, in the city of Columbus, on the 29th. He will appoint his own aides, and will have entire control of the ceremonies and procession attending the transfer of the remains from and to the depot.

"All societies, delegations, or other organizations, wishing to participate in the ceremonies, will report, by telegraph or letter, to the Chief Marshall on or before ten o' clock of Friday the 28th.

"The headquarters of the Chief Marshal, during Thursday and Friday, 27th and 28th, will be at the Adjutant General's office, in the Capitol."

Hardly had the train stopped in Columbus when the entire operation of dealing with the Presidential remains went into effect. Carriages were waiting, three abreast, for the funeral party. The coffin was efficiently conveyed to a specially constructed, dramatic-looking hearse, which was 17 feet long, 8 and a half feet wide. It stood 17 and a half feet tall from the ground to the top of the majestic canopy.

The floor of the hearse was four feet above the ground. A dais was raised two and a half feet above the floor, making it overall six and a half feet above the street. Above all this, the coffin rested, where it was breathtaking in its elevation for all to see it. The canopy was formed like a Chinese pagoda. The interior of the canopy was lined with silk flags. The outside was covered with black broadcloth.

Scene of the Lincoln Funeral procession in Columbus, Ohio, where thousands lined the streets to pay tribute. Later the remains were moved further by train to Indianapolis, Indiana. *Prints and Photographs Division, Library of Congress.*

Meanwhile, the dais, the main floor of the hearse, and the entire hearse itself was covered with black cloth, which hung in festoons from the main platform to within a few inches of the ground. The broadcloth was then fringed with silver lace and further ornamented with heavy tassels of black silk.

Surrounding the cornice were 36 silver stars, and on the apex and the four corners were heavy black plumes. The canopy was amazingly curtained with black cloth and lined with a sheep's wool white merino to provide a cashmere-like effect. Spectators could read the name "Lincoln" on each side of the dais in large silver letters.

Finally the magnificent hearse was drawn by six white horses. Each horse was covered with black plumes. Each horse was led by a groom who was dressed in black, wearing white gloves with a white band around each groom's hat.

Now the procession was moving down the streets of Columbus. The crowd of spectators was immense, starting at the depot and fanning out along the route. Bands assembled periodically, and with the military, and other marchers played solemnly. One viewer called the procession "the most imposing which ever marched through the streets of Columbus. The slow measured tread of the troops, the muffled drums, the dead march, the enshrouded colors all told their own tale of the fearfully mournful occasion on which they were passing in review before the assembled thousands who had congregated as witnesses."

Winding its way to the State Capitol building those in the procession could occasionally hear the booming cannon and tolling bells in the distance. Presently the building of their destination came into view "The pillars of that beautiful white edifice were artistically draped in mourning," wrote one observer at the scene, "and flags were at half-mast on each side of the dome. A banner was displayed conspicuously, in large black letters." That banner read: "With malice toward none, with charity for all."

First National Bank of Columbus (Ohio) is decorated and draped in mourning while President Lincoln is lying in state at the Ohio Statehouse nearby. Taken in April of 1865. *Prints and Photographs Division, Library of Congress.*

Still another banner arched over the grate leading to the grounds of the State Capitol and proclaimed, "Ohio Mourns." Over the entrance to the building itself was still another banner, "God Moves in a Mysterious Way."

Steadily the coffin was conveyed into the rotunda, where it was deposited on a mound of moss "thickly dotted" with the choicest of flowers, and surrounded by equally elegant vases of rare exotic flowers.

"The walls were adorned with clusters of battle flags," according to one onlooker, "torn and riddle with bullets, as they were borne by Ohio regiments in suppressing the rebellion. These were festooned with crepe, and drooped sadly around the spacious rotunda."

As the coffin was opened, there was a stunning silence among those who filled the area. The assigned caretakers who had traveled with the remains on the train since Washington worked briefly to rearrange the body. "Instructions were given more by signs than words," later wrote one correspondent, "and arrangements were made for people to look upon the remains."

Mrs. Lucy Hoffner, representing the Horticultural Society of Cincinnati, the only woman present, stepped softly forward and placed at the foot of the coffin an anchor composed of delicate white flowers and evergreen boughs. She placed a small wreath upon the chest of Lincoln and a cross just above his head.

A hushed crowd began filing by the coffin. "There was no stiffness to jar the softened feeling," noted one writer, "no unwanted display to mar the solemnity, but beautiful and simply grand was the character of him whose mortal remains were to repose therein, the rotunda of Ohio's Capitol became the emblem of sorrow for Ohio's people."

In the afternoon a ceremony was held on the east side of the capitol building. On one stage was Major General Joseph Hooker and Major General David Hunter, along with members of the clergy from Columbus and surrounding areas. Hooker, ever the Civil War icon, was greeted with cheers and cries of tribute as he rose to address the crowd: "My friends, I thank you very much for the compliment you pay me by your call. If I do not respond by remarks, you will ascribe it to the inappropriateness of the occasion. Your call was dictated by curiosity as much as to hear a speech from me: that I grant you. Further you must excuse me."

Hunter was another crowd favorite who had little to say at the time.

Sometimes known as "Black Dave" he had seen action as early as the First Battle of Bull Run. Hunter had caused controversy first by advocating arming slaves (African Americans) from occupied districts of South Carolina. In keeping with that cause, he formed the first Union Army Regiment, 1st South Carolina for those of African descent.

Later, he caused another controversy by issuing an order emancipating the slaves in Georgia, South Carolina, and Florida.

Despite all this, or maybe because of this, General Hunter was specifically chosen by Secretary of War Stanton to be a part of the Honor Guard that would accompany President Lincoln's body on the entire train journey from Washington to Springfield.

Still, General Hunter was mostly quiet at the Columbus ceremony.

Possibly the most eloquent speech of the day at the rotunda in Columbus was presented by local lawmaker Job E. Stevenson. According to one journalist, Stevenson addressed the "vast assemblage, in a most thrilling oration. He was listened to with the most profound attention from beginning to end." The Republican state senator would eventually be elected to the United States Congress following the Civil War, but when the funeral train halted in Columbus, he was known as a regional legislator and keen public speaker. Born in the middle of nowhere in Yellow Bud, Ohio, he went on to become a successful lawyer in Chillicothe, Ohio.

"Ohio mourns, America mourns, and the civilized world will mourn the cruel death of Abraham Lincoln, the brave, the wise, the good; bravest, wisest, best of men," he told the crowd there that afternoon. "History alone can measure and weight his worth, but we, in parting from his mortal remains, may indulge the fullness of our hearts, in a few broken words, of his life, his death, and his fame."

Stevenson went on to impart the following to the mourners: "He stood on the summit, his brow bathed in the beams of the rising sum of peace, singing in his heart the angelic song Glory to God in the highest, peace on earth and good will toward man. With malice toward none, with charity for all, he had forgiven the people of the South, and might have forgiven their leaders—covering the broad mantle of his charity their multitude of sins. But he is slain—slain by slavery. That fiend incarnate did the deed. Beaten in battle, the leaders sought to save slavery by assassination. This madness presaged their destruction.

"Abraham Lincoln was the personification of mercy. Andrew Johnson is the personification of justice. They have murdered mercy, and justice rules alone and the people, with one voice, pray to heaven that justice will be done. The blood of thousands of murdered prisoners cries to heaven. The shades of sixty-two thousand starved soldiers rise up in judgment against them. The body of the murdered President condemns them."

And then Stevenson concluded: "The imperial free Republic, the best and strongest government on earth, will be a monument to his glory, while over and above all shall rise and swell the great dome of his fame."

A long line of mourners were still waiting that evening, even through as one account observed, "thousands of men, women and children visited and revisited the catafalque, and again and again with sad emotions viewed the symbols of grief which decorated the rotunda of Ohio's Capitol."

The proud procession of that morning in Columbus was re-formed, and as such, escorted the remains to the depot. At 8 p.m. the funeral train was ready to resume its steady course.

The Lincoln Funeral Train departed from Columbus in the darkness, but with some different railroad executives aboard. This time among the passengers was B. E. Smith, president of the Columbus and Indianapolis Railway, and J.M. Hunt, superintendent of the Columbus and Indianapolis Railway. They were reported to be "giving personal attention to the wants and wishes of passengers."

The locomotive Old Nashville, which pulled the Lincoln Funeral Train through much of Ohio in April of 1865. Vintage postcard, estimated $20–$30.

Riding with chiefs of this particular rail line was a veteran crew, which included William Slater, telegraphic operator "with all the necessary implements for immediate repair," conductor S. A. Hughes, and engineer James Gounley. Bonfires were again lighting the black night as the train rolled very so slowly into Pleasant Valley. Besides the crowd gathered at the depot, there were two ladies holding two large American flags draped in mourning.

At Unionville, the awaiting assembly of about 200 people drew a brief note from a correspondent who commented, "most of them (were) sitting in wagons—the people having come in from the country."

A crowd of about 500 were gathered in the darkness at the depot in Woodstock. The time was around 9:30 p.m. This was a full stop, and two groups of ladies, ten women in all, would be allowed to board the train and distribute fresh flowers. The first group was identified in part as including Miss Ann Villard, Miss Lucy Kimble, and Miss Mary Cranston, "on the part of the Ladies of Woodstock." Another group with flowers included sisters, Mrs. G. Martin and Miss Delilah Beltz.

While the ceremonies with flowers and two groups of women was going on, the Woodstock Comet Band, led by U. Cushman, played assorted hymns including, "Dreaming, I Sleep, Love." There was the typical gathering who had braved the dark and rainy night at the next station, Cable. Standing out from the crowd and the bonfires, however, was an American soldier in full uniform holding an American flag.

It was 10:40 p.m. when the funeral train finally reached Urbana. Estimates put the Urbana mourners at somewhere over 3,000 people. Most of them were assembled around one huge bonfire. On the train platform at the depot was a large cross entwined with circling wreaths of evergreens. The piece was said to be the work of Mrs. Milo G. Williams, who was president of the Ladies' Soldiers' Aide Society.

On the opposite side of the track at the Urbana station was an elevated platform that held a cluster of 40 men and women singing "patriotic sweetness" including the hymn, "Go To Thy Rest." At nearly the same time a group of ten young ladies entered the hearse car to once again add fresh flowers to coffin bearing President Lincoln. An observer later wrote, "one of the ladies was so affected that she cried and wept in great anguish."

At the Westville Station, there were two long lines of people waiting to greet the funeral train. In one line were little boys and girls, and younger men and women. In the other line were elderly people. In the center of it all was a large American flag held by three young ladies—Miss Eliza Throckmorton, Miss Nora Brecount, and Miss Rebecca Barnes.

"A patriotic religious song, with a slow and mournful air, was chanted by the flag bears," noted one present on the train.

Both the Troy Band and the Pique Band were playing mournful music when the funeral train finally arrived in Piqua. The time was 12:20 a.m., and despite the chill of a very, very early Sunday, a crowd of more than 10,000 spectators was awaiting the train. After a brief musical interlude by the bands, the Methodist choir under the direction of Reverend Granville Moody performed. Rev. Moody read each line before it was then sung by the entire choir. One such line was: "Think of such actions at the midnight hour, when humanity is supposed to lay by its cares, and take its rest in the arms of repose."

Covington, Bradford Junction, and then Gettysburg "were passed in quick succession," it was reported, "and, notwithstanding it was in the middle of the night, there was a large crowd at each place, with bonfires, flags and mottoes." Still another account mentioned specifically Gettysburg, noting large numbers of uncounted people there.

At 2 a.m. on Sunday, April 30, 1865 the train arrived at Greenville.

A group of 36 ladies dressed in white stood waving the Star Spangled Banner as the funeral train slowed to a halt at the Greenville

Ohio schoolhouse draped for the funeral of President Lincoln in 1865. Identified as the Butler School and published by the Bryan Post Card Company in Bryan, Ohio. Vintage real photo postcard, estimated $20–$25.

station. Some 500 citizens were gathered along with the entire Company C of the 28th Ohio Infantry, which stood at attention with fires reversed. Standing nearby were a group of men and women, possibly a choir, who softly sang Lafayette's Requiem.

The entire scene at Greenville was brilliantly revealed in the night by the light of two 15-foot high bonfires burning brightly. There was also a massive archway standing 20 feet tall and expanding to about 30 feet around.

At Wiley's, New Madison, and Weaver's Station, "hundreds of mourners were congregated," according to one account.

On Sunday at 2:41 a.m., the train reached New Paris. One writer left this notation regarding the New Paris passing: "The depot was artistically draped in the mourning. Arch spanned the track. It was adorned by evergreens draped in mourning. The scene was lighted up by bonfires.

"This is the last town on that line of road in the State of Ohio."

Thus the Lincoln Funeral Train departed the state and the spirit of 1860s Ohio.

Crowds in places like Cleveland and Columbus were of course impressive. But the turnout in the rural areas along the normally deserted byways was awesome. Some who rode the train said the night sky was almost continuously lit by the lingering torches and bonfires of countless thousands.

This was the engine Louisville, operating chiefly on the Cleveland, Columbus, and Cincinnati Railroad. It served as the pilot train for the Lincoln Funeral Train in parts of Ohio and as the main engine for the train in much of Indiana. *Prints and Photographs Division, Library of Congress.*

This was the schedule for Ohio:

(FRIDAY, APRIL 28, 1865)
Conneaut arrive 3:47a.m.
Amboy
Kingville
Ashtabula arrive 4:27 a.m.
Saybrook
Geneva
Unionville
Madison
Perry
Lane
Painesville
Heisley
Mentor
Reynolds
Willoughby arrive 6:08 a.m.
Rushroad
Wickliffe arrive 6:20 a.m.
Euclid
Noble
Nottingham
Collinwood
Colits
Glenville
Cleveland arrive 7 a.m. depart 12 p.m.

(SATURDAY, APRIL 29, 1865)
West Park
Berea
Olmstead
Columbia
North Eaton
Grafton
LaGrange
Wellington
Rochester
New London
Greenwich
Shiloh
Vernon
Crestline arrive 4 a.m.
Galion
Iberia (St. James)
Gilead (Edison)
Cardington arrive 5 :20 a.m.
Ashley

Eden (Leoardsburg)
Delaware
Berlin
Lewis Center
Orange
Flint
Worthington
Columbus arrive 7 a.m. depart 8 p.m.
Scioto (Grand View)
Mounds
Marble Cliff
Hillards
Bronson's (Hyden)
Pleasant Valley (Plain City) arrive
8:45 p.m.
Unionville arrive 9 p.m.
Milford Center arrive 9: 12 p.m.
Woodstock
Fountaine Park
Brush Lake
Cable arrive 10: 13 p.m.
Hagenbaugh
Urbana arrive 10:40 pm.
Rice
Westville (McGrew)
St. Paris arrive 11 :24 p.m.
Lena
Conover arrive 11 :30 p.m.
Fletcher arrive 12 p.m.

(SUNDAY, APRIL 30, 1865)
Spring Creek
Jordan
Piqua arrive 12:20 a.m.
Summit
Union City (Bradford)
Gettysburg arrive 1: 1 0 a.m.
New Harrison
Greenville arrive 1 :36 a.m.
Weaver's Station
New Madison
New Paris arrive 2:41 a.m.

For the first time in its historic journey the Lincoln Funeral Train would be crossing into a state where the President had actually lived—when it crossed into the boundaries of Indiana.

Lincoln had moved to Indiana from Kentucky during his eighth year. He grew up in the wilds of Spencer County and learned to read by candlelight in a primitive cabin there. His beloved mother, Nancy Hanks Lincoln, was buried in the rustic countryside of this state.

Young Abraham Lincoln had left Indiana as a gangling young man. He was returning as a man who had occupied the office of the Presidency. At six feet four inches, he was the tallest person to be president, and as a true Midwesterner, he was the first president to have been born and raised outside of the original 13 Colonies.

On April 27, while the train bearing Lincoln's remains was still proceeding through the state of New York, the *New Castle* (Indiana) *Courier* published this notice for its readers—many of which lived near or within a wagon's ride from the Central Railroad tracks: "The remains of our

Portrait by Matthew Wilson

ABRAHAM LINCOLN

Painting of President Abraham Lincoln reportedly completed by Connecticut portrait artist Matthew Wilson in April of 1865 after Lincoln had sat for him in February of that year. Secretary of the Navy Gideon Wells, who commissioned the painting, paid the artist $85 for the work on April 12, 1865—just two days before the President was assassinated. The original painting ended up at the Lincoln Museum in Fort Wayne, Indiana.

The tomb of Nancy Hanks Lincoln, the mother of President Abraham Lincoln, is depicted in an early postcard at what is now known as the Lincoln Boyhood National Memorial in Lincoln City, Indiana. Real photo postcard, estimated $3–$5.

late President will pass over the Central Railroad and be received at Indianapolis at 7 o'clock on next Sunday morning the 30th.

"The largest crowd that ever assembled at the Capitol of our State is expected at that time, and great preparations are being made for the occasion. We believe all the Railroads will carry passengers on extra trains at reduced prices."

That very same edition also carried two other news items of interest to their readers. One was that peace negotiations were underway in a region of North Carolina with General Joseph Johnson, commanding officer of the Confederate Army, and General W.T. Sherman, commanding officer of the Army of the United States.

The other incident was closer to home and suggested some very strong feelings regarding the death of President Lincoln: "Five soldiers were hung by their comrades until almost dead, at Indianapolis, for rejoicing over the assassination of the President.

"Some citizens of Middletown expressed their disgust for a 'refugee' who expressed gratification at the crime, by tarring and feathering him, and other delicate attentions.

"In Prairie township, we learn of some 'Sons' openly rejoicing as might not have been expected over the National calamity."

It was shortly after 3 a.m. Sunday morning, April 30, when the train rolled in to Richmond, the first town across the Ohio-Indiana border.

Arrangements had been made the day before to have all bells, including church bells, ringing in the community an hour prior to the arrival of the funeral cortege. They were to continue ringing as the train halted at the depot.

It must have sounded somewhat strange, and eye-witness accounts confirmed it: "At the time appointed they pealed forth their notes on the still night air," said one, "and soon the streets were filled with men and women, old and young, all wending their way to the depot."

"Not only were the city bells tolling as the train arrived," noted another, "but there were bells tolling on the engines of other trains at the crossroad, along with revolving lamps."

Glen Miller Park. RICHMOND, Ind.

An early postcard scene shows horse-driven carriages and visitors, in Miller Park at Richmond, Indiana. Vintage postcard published by W. H. Bartel Jr. of Richmond, Indiana. Estimated $3–$5.

Broad-brimmed hats and Quaker bonnets "were liberally sprinkled among the vast concourse—as Friends (Quakers) are more numerous here, in proportion to the whole population, than they are in the city of Philadelphia."

Crowd estimates were that despite a time when the good folks of this region would be home in bed there must have been 12,000 to 15,000 people filling the streets. "The whole population of the city came out," according to one report, "and the people in the surrounding country left their homes in the middle of the night and came many miles in wagons, carriages, and on horseback."

There were major decorations in Richmond too. A spectacular arch was constructed above the track that stood 25 feet tall and was 30 feet wide. As the funeral train passed under the arch, there were American flags posted on both sides of the track arranged in triangles. Down the sides of them were transparencies (see-through textiles) of red, white, and blue. Beyond that were chaplets (wreaths or garlands) of evergreens complete with velvet rosettes.

Across from the mighty arch was a large platform, about 18 feet from the base. It was carpeted with black velvet. At the ends of the platform were two flags in drooping folds. In the center of the platform was a female representing the Goddess of Liberty. She was in a sitting position, weeping over a coffin. On one side was a boy-soldier, and on the other side was a boy-sailor. Both acted as mourners for Miss Liberty.

Indiana governor Oliver P. Morton, described by one correspondent as "a warm personal friend of the deceased President," had arrived on a special train from Indianapolis earlier. He brought with him a group of nearly 100 state officials and elected office-holders to pay respects to the fallen leader.

Morton was serving as the 14th governor of the state, and had reign a controversial term during the Civil War. When the war first erupted in April of 1861, he had telegraphed Lincoln that the state already had 10,000 soldiers under arms to fight for the Union.

Lincoln was reported to once have said of Morton, he was "at times the shrewdest person I know." Morton was credited with being most active in supporting Lincoln's ultimate signing of the Emancipation Proclamation.

Morton was accompanied on the trip to Richmond by Lt. Governor Conrad Baker, state auditor T. B. McCarty, and state treasurer John I. Morrison. Also in the distinguished group that very early Sunday morning was Senator Thomas Hendricks, a man who would someday be Vice President of the United States.

Hendricks, a former Congressman and leader in the Democrat party, was elected to the U.S. Senate by the Indiana General Assembly. He took office in 1863 and would continue there for several years. Decades later, in 1884, Hendricks was elected to national office with running mate and then President Grover Cleveland.

For all of its decorative splendor and for all of its notable visitors and its obscure masses of mourners, the train's stay at Richmond was relatively short. "After a brief pause, the train moved slowly away, and the multitude, with sad hearts, dispersed to their homes in silence," witnessed one at the scene.

At 3:41 a.m., the train pulled into Centerville, Indiana. "The depot at Centerville was splendidly robed in mourning," wrote one observer. Among the details were two chandeliers gleaming radiantly at each end of the railroad platform.

Centerville was the home of Congressman George W. Julian, a former Whig like Lincoln who had eventually moved on to the Republican Party. At one point in his political career, Julian was nominated as a Vice President candidate on the Free-Soil ticket with presidential candidate John Hale. The effort was unsuccessful, but did garner more than 155,000 votes nationally. Julian was a supporter of women's right to vote and a few years after Lincoln's death he would propose a constitutional amendment towards that end.

Again, despite an attentive and somber crowd the train's stop was brief. "The people were anxious for the train to tarry longer," noted one correspondent, "but of course their wishes could not be complied with."

Observers noted "a number of brilliant bonfires" across the landscape as the train passed through Germantown. The time was 4:05 a.m. Sunday.

Long before the funeral train reached Cambridge City, the sounds of artillery firing salvos could be heard. On the horizon was also the growing glow of blue lights.

"Eventually the darkness turned into a solemn glare by the burning of Bengal lights (flare-like lights that glowed like fireworks), and the reddish blue met the first streaks of grey on the eastern horizon," commented one writer, "the effect was solemn and impressive."

A view of *The Cambridge City Tribune* as it was celebrating the passage of the Lincoln Funeral Train there a century earlier. This is the April 26, 1928 issue of the newspaper noting, "artillery salutes marked its arrival at dawn, April 30, 1865."

Others were equally impressed with the Cambridge City scene.

"It was the unanimous verdict of those who traveled on all the journey with the train, that this, and the display at Richmond," wrote one, "was not excelled in taste and appropriateness by anything that had been witnessed."

"There was a solemn earnestness depicted on the countenance of the Indiana patriots," one added, "and the sentence seemed to be written as if in burnished rows of steel, that through Lincoln had died, the republic should live."

At Dublin, people were standing everywhere.

The platform and both sides of the track were lined with citizens. It was hard to know for sure, but it appeared that every one of the town's residents seemed to be standing there in silence in the early morning rain. It was 4:27 a.m.

"Their looks and actions," noted an observer, "bespoke their deep grief."

Dublin was the last train stop in Wayne County. During the Presidential election of 1864, not that much earlier from this fateful night, the election results came in to the county seat in Richmond. Dublin voted 269 for President Lincoln and zero for his opponent, General George McClellan, as noted in the book's introduction.

"There has never been a whiskey-shop in the town (Dublin), and it's not a remarkable coincidence that for many years the Republican ticket has been voted unanimously," one traveling writer said, "not a single one on the other side."

Observers at the time credited the town's nature much to the Quaker influence, despite its obvious Irish heritage name. "And, although you would see little of the outward sign of that particular people," wrote a journalist, "their principles are nowhere more decidedly felt than in this place."

Like so many other places along the way, passengers on the funeral train would notice Dublin's very neat, evergreen-entwined arch, a large American flag draped on the depot, and the distinctive portrait of President Lincoln.

The next stop was at the village of Lewisville. There, a group of ladies boarded with fresh flowers, and a group of leaflets they distributed among the passengers.

Each leaflet read the same:

> We mingle our tears with yours.
> Lincoln! The Savior of his country; the emancipator of a Race, and the Friend of all Mankind.
> Triumphs over Death, and mounts Victoriously upward with his old familiar tread.

The stations were Raysville and Knightstown where it was reported "mourning emblems and other demonstrations of sorrow were everywhere visible." At Knightstown, there were arches erected at each end of the depot. Citizens had also "festooned the depot building itself with badges of sorrow."

At 5:40 a.m., the train slowed for Charlottesville.

The sight prompted this report later from the *Indianapolis Daily Journal*: "The little village had not forgotten that the honored dead was a friend of the oppressed, and chief among the procession at the depot was quite a large body of colored people.

"How fitting and sublime seemed the gospel declaration, as the Great Emancipator's coffin passed through a file of free men, Of one blood made He all nation's men."

The train slowed to a near stop for those gathered at Cleveland, and moved on steadily toward Greenfield. Around 5:55 a.m. the train was within sight of a watchman waiting atop the roof of the depot in Greenfield. At that point the watchman began alerting the crowd below and the sounding of bells began.

One written account described the waiting crowd in the small town as "overflowing." There is speculation that future Hoosier poet, James Whitcomb Riley, may have been among them. Riley would

This is the home of Hoosier poet James Whitcomb Riley, in Greenfield, Indiana, as shown in an early postcard. The Lincoln Funeral Train passed through very near here when Riley was a youngster. Vintage postcard image.

have been a teenager when the Lincoln train passed through, and lived only a short distance from the rail station.

After Greenfield, there was another brief pause at the station in Cumberland before the train moved into Indianapolis.

The time was 7 a.m. It was raining heavily.

During the previous 24 hours, busy train traffic had brought thousands of passengers into the city to mourn the remains of President Lincoln. Great numbers had also arrived by the standard carriages, buggies, and wagons. In addition, there was the residential population—turning out in masses.

With the train finally at the depot, the Indianapolis City Band began mournfully playing, "Lincoln's Funeral March." In the distance was the sound of firing artillery and the tolling of countless church bells.

A local guard of soldiers helped move the casket to a large hearse especially prepared for the occasion. The hearse was drawn by eight white horses, six of whom had been attached to the carriage that President Lincoln had been riding during a stopover four years earlier on the way to Washington.

The Lincoln Funeral Train stopped in Indianapolis during the early morning of April 30, 1865. Lincoln's body was then transported by hearse to the Indiana Statehouse shown here. Vintage postcard, $2–$4.

Each horse wore a black velvet cover, and each bore a black and white plume.

The hearse itself was topped with an eagle in the center with a silver gilt. The sides of the hearse were studded with silver stars.

"The avenues leading to the depot were closely packed with people," according to one report, even as the heavy rain continued. Steadily the rain-soaked procession made its way from the rail station to the State House.

Along the way the city, streets were extensively decorated in the mood of sadness.

"All the streets bore badges and emblems of mourning, but Washington Street presented superior display," wrote one present. "At all interesting streets were triple arches, adorned in part with evergreens and national flags, arranged in the most tasteful and beautiful manner."

The State House Square was hung with wreaths and other decorations in a most impressive manner. There was a large structure, "combining a variety of styles of architecture." It stood about 21 feet high, 40 feet long, and 24 feet wide. Underneath was a carriage-way 12 feet wide, with six-foot passage on either side.

At the State House structure, the main pillars stood 15 feet high. Portraits of General U.S. Grant, General William Sherman, and Governor Oliver Morton were suspended from the pillars. On the pedestals at the top rested magnificent busts of George Washington, Daniel Webster, Abraham Lincoln, and Henry Clay.

The entire structure of the State House was shrouded in black and white, and in addition there were evergreens and a sweeping display of flags. At the north side was simple gothic arch, "with the usual draping." At the south side were pillars covered with alternating black and white cloth and edged in evergreens. In the center of them was the Indiana State coat of arms.

Presently the body of President Lincoln was unloaded from the hearse, placed in the interior of the State House, and made ready for viewing. A bust of Lincoln, by T.D. Jones of Cincinnati, stood on a pedestal at the head of the coffin, the brow of it was encircled by a laurel wreath.

The hall itself was contained in black cloth, and was brilliantly lighted with numerous chandeliers. The catafalque, on which the coffin rested was covered with black velvet and trimmed with silver fringe. Above the catafalque was a pagoda-like canopy with black material and white cords and tassels. The ceiling was decorated with golden stars.

Awaiting the arrival of the Lincoln Funeral hearse, the Indiana State Capitol building is heavily decorated in mourning. Vintage postcard, $5–$10.

State Capitol, Indianapolis, Indiana, During Funeral of Abraham Lincoln

The Lincoln horse-drawn hearse surrounded by mourners is shown the day after the funeral event in Indianapolis, Indiana. Heavy rains on the day of the funeral forced the enactment. *Prints and Photographs Division, Library of Congress.*

Others braved the weather anyway.

"The colored Masons, in their appropriate clothing, and colored citizens generally turned out and visited the remains in a body," noted an observer. Some of the banners that the group carried were: "Colored Men always Loyal", "Lincoln, Martyr of Liberty," "He Lives in our Memories," and "Slavery is Dead."

All day and into the night they streamed into the Indiana State House building to pay tribute to President Lincoln. By nightfall, hundreds stood outside holding torches aloft, casting an eerie light upon the sight of waiting lines.

It was estimated that people passed the coffin there at the rate of 150 per minute. Furthermore, there were published reports that upwards of 100,000 citizens passed by the body of Lincoln. There had been elaborate preparations for a civic and military procession from the coffin-bound hearse to the train depot, but the deluge of rain interfered. General William Hovey finally gave orders that the procession not be formed.

Meanwhile, the coffin, as it rested upon the dais, was surrounded by flowers. The Veteran Reserve bearers added a white wreath with floral crosses.

A nearby choir began singing a funeral hymn.

The first watch of the Indianapolis Guard of Honor had begun at 7 a.m. It would last two hours. The Guard included Colonel J.S. Simson, Major C.S. Stevenson, Paymaster A.D. Gall, Captain T. Teneyck, Captain S.A. Craig, and Captain W.H. Thompson.

Among the first to view the remains around 9 a.m. were Sunday-school children, next were ladies in the throng gathered outside, and finally regular citizens.

According to accounts at the time, the rather intense rain not only marred much of the decorations around the State House and elsewhere in Indianapolis, but also disrupted some of the planned attendance by organizations.

Another view of the Indiana State House heavily decorated in preparation for the arrival of the remains from the Lincoln Funeral Train. *Prints and Photographs Division, Library of Congress.*

Sheet music cover of the Funeral March to the Memory of Abraham Lincoln, published by Oliver Ditson and Company in Boston. It was one of many funeral marches and songs published at the time of Lincoln's death.

Arch decoration in tribute to President Abraham Lincoln over the tracks at Michigan City, Indiana. *Prints and Photographs Division, Library of Congress.*

The *Indiana Journal* reported it this way:

"The unpropitious weather prevented the funeral pageant, but an offset to the disappointment of the people in this was the increased facility given to view the remains as they lay in state at the Capitol. Even Indiana may feel that the honor of the State has been brightened rather than compromised by their reception of the remains of President Lincoln, and the State where he passed some years of his youth, has rendered her full quota of honor to him as Savior of his Country."

At around 10 p.m. a parade of marshals encircled the casket and it was formally closed. The remains were rendered back onto the casket for the trip back in the darkness to the train depot. Many mourners followed, bearing their torches to light the way.

The Lincoln Funeral Train left Indianapolis at midnight.

There were what one account described as "formidable demonstrations" held in the middle of the night at various places, which included Augusta, Zionsville, Whitestown, Lebanon, Hazelrigg, Thorntown, Colfax, Stockwell, and "many other points."

"The depots were draped in mourning and other insignia of sorrow was visible, in the light of bonfires and torches," said one observer, "but the people were assembled in large numbers at every point, to witness the Great Funeral Train."

It was 3:35 a.m. on Monday, May 1, when the train reached Lafayette.

Among the passengers came this observation: "It was known that the train would stop at this place but a few minutes, but it appeared to those on board as if all the inhabitants of the city, and from many miles of surrounding country, were there. The depot was draped in mourning, and the surrounding scene well lighted. The bells were tolled, and other manifestations of sorrow were visible."

From Lafayette, the stations of Tippecanoe Battle Ground, Bookston, Chalmers, Reynolds, Bradford, Francisville, Medaryville, Kankakee, La Crosse, Wanatha, Westville, Lacroix, and many other towns were draped, "and the people in many ways demonstrated their sorrow for the loss of our chief magistrate, "according to one later published account.

Its last major stop before Chicago would be Michigan City. It arrived there at 8 a.m. that Monday morning.

Shown here is the arrival scene of the Lincoln Funeral Train beneath a decorative arch at Michigan City, Indiana. The time was shortly after 8 a.m. on May 1, 1865. *Prints and Photographs Division, Library of Congress.*

The funeral train had been heading steadily northward since leaving Indianapolis and now was at the upper most boundary of Indiana at the shore of Lake Michigan.

Michigan City was to be the site of a tremendous breakfast feast, which would not only include the funeral party aboard the train and local officials, but members of the Chicago Citizens Committee of 100 as well.

Representatives of the prominent Committee of 100 had met to plan their part in this event back when the train was in Cleveland, Ohio. They had taken a special train earlier from Chicago in order to meet the funeral train. Unlike the funeral train itself, the Chicago Committee of 100 special would include both female and African-American passengers.

The special Chicago train also included the powerful U.S. House of Representatives speaker of the house, Schuyler Colfax. Colfax was an old ally for President Lincoln and was said to be one of the last conferees to meet with the President on the day Lincoln was assassinated. Some accounts even suggest Colfax had been invited by the President to attend the theatre with President Lincoln and Mrs. Lincoln, but the imminent legislator had declined.

Colfax and Lincoln had been avid members of the Whig Party at one time, but both eventually joined the "new" Republican Party. Colfax had a noble future in his political party and in the nation. He would eventually serve as Vice President with President Ulysses S. Grant. Grant at 46 and Colfax at 45 would be the youngest presidential team in history at the time later in the 19th century.

Meanwhile, the "bountiful breakfast" event was underway in Michigan City.

While guests were breakfasting in the main station house, a group of 36 young ladies, representing the 36 States of the Union, and another representing the Goddess of Liberty, appeared in "appropriate costumes."

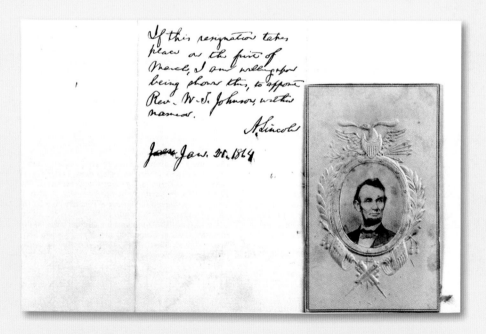

Note signed by President Lincoln on a one page, six-line docket response to a letter from William Reese to Reverend William Johnson, resigning form his post. It reads, "If this resignation takes place on the first of March, I am willing upon being shown this, to appoint Rev. W.J. Johnson, within named. A. Lincoln." Together with a period embossed paper carte. *Skinner, Inc.*, estimated $7,000–$9,000.

Nearby a group of 16 ladies, led by Miss Mary Colfax, the niece of Congressman Colfax, then entered the funeral car. While guns fired and music sounded in the distance, the group placed fresh flowers upon President Lincoln's coffin.

The Michigan City depot itself was decorated in mourning, and a triple arch covered track. The arch was marked with a large flag "bearing the national colors" at half-mast. Portraits of Lincoln were suspended from the center of arch, "wreathed in evergreens, and surrounded by draped flags and other insignia of sorrow."

Among the mourning signs displayed there were:

"Nobelest martyr to Freedom; sacred thy dust; hallowed thy resting place."

1809-1865

Postcard marking the birth and death of Abraham Lincoln, facsimile of his signature. First printing by W.M. Grady, Warner, New Hampshire.

"With tears we resign thee to God and History."

"Our guiding star has fallen; our nation mourns."

"Though dead he yet speaketh."

Now it was again time to move on to nearby Illinois.

"After all had partaken of breakfast," a passenger later noted, "the train started for Chicago, at 8:35 a.m., over the Michigan Central Railroad."

A few days later, the *New Castle Courier* published the following news item:

"The funeral precession of our late loved President, exceeded in solemn grandeur anything of the sort ever witnessed in this country, or perhaps in the world.

"Everything along the route of over a thousand miles, at every village and hamlet, the people turned out with emblems and decorations of mourning to testify their share in sorrow, and appreciation of the worth of the illustrious dead.

"At the State Line the funeral train was met and escorted to the Capitol by a special train containing the Governor, state officials, and many distinguished citizens. All along the Central road a suitable display was made, the citizens of Lewisville, Coffin's Station, Ogden, Raysville, and Knightstown vying with others.

Arriving at Indianapolis on Sunday morning, the train was received by an immense throng of people, and although the day on account of the incessant rain was rendered one of the most disagreeable, the decoration of the city was grand and imposing, scarce surpassed at the other point."

It is estimated that at least 100,000 persons were enabled to behold for the last time, the face of one who has endeared himself to the people as no other man has done.

This was the schedule for Indiana:

(SUNDAY, APRIL 30, 1865)
Richmond arrive 3 a.m.
Centerville arrive 3:41 a.m.
Harvey's

Germantown arrive 4:05 a.m.
Cambridge City arrive 4:15 a.m.
Dublin arrive 4:27 a.m.
Straughn's
Lewisville
Coffin's (Dunreith)
Ogden
Rayville
Knightstown
Charlottesville arrive 5:40 a.m.
Cleveland
Greenfield
Philadelphia
Cumberland
Engine House (Thorne)
Indianapolis arrive 7 a.m. depart
12 p.m.

(MONDAY, MAY 1, 1865)
Augusta
Zionsville
Whitestown
Lebanon
Hazelrigg
Thorntown
Colfax
Clark's Hill
Stockwell
Culvier's Station
Lafayette Junction

Lafayette arrive 3:20 a.m.
Tippecanoe Battleground
Brookston
Chalmers
Reynolds
Bradford (Monon)
Francisville
Kankakee
Medaryville
San Pierre
Wilders
La Crosse
Wanatag
Haskells
Alida
Westville
LaCroix (Otis)
Michigan City arrive 8 a.m. depart
8:35 p.m.
Furnassville
Kensington

Signed one-page document by President Lincoln appointing William Hagadorn as Second Lieutenant in the Veterans Reserve Corps, countersigned by Secretary of War Edwin Stanton. The document is about 19 inches by 15 inches with light fading and overall wear. *Skinner, Inc.,* estimated $3,500–$5,000.

Homeland

(Illinois)

"Today the city in which he was nominated President of the United States is gathered together to bury him."

—*Chicago Tribune*, May 1, 1865.

No one knows the actual size of the mass of people that came to Chicago for the arrival of the Lincoln Funeral Train and the procession and viewing that immediately followed.

Some accounts say it was at least 100,000. Other reports suggest it could have been 250,000. It was, by any measure, historic for the city of Chicago and the state of Illinois.

Oval albumenized salt print of Abraham Lincoln attributed to Roderick M. Cole or Henry M. Cole. It is inscribed in pencil, H. H. Cole, 1859, Peoria, Illinois. Image is about 7 inches by 5 inches and mounted. This Lincoln image was widely reproduced on campaign ribbons of the 1860 presidential campaign although its origins are disputed. Cole's brother, Roderick, wrote to a founder of the Illinois State Historical Library, a repository of Lincoln's papers, that the photograph was made in "my gallery in (Peoria) during the Lincoln and Douglas campaign." *Swann Galleries*, estimated $4,000–$5,000.

Lincoln Funeral Train crossing at the lakefront at Michigan City in Indiana heading for the Illinois state line and ultimately a stop in Chicago. The Lincoln hearse car near the end of the train is not visible in this picture. *Prints and Photographs Division, Library of Congress.*

It was near 11 a.m. that Monday when the train arrived outskirts of Chicago and pulled in sight of Lake Calumet. At the time Lake Calumet remained just to the south of the city in a swampy area of Hyde Park Township. There was already an enormous crowd of people there, along with squads of soldiers stationed on the hillsides.

"As the funeral train neared Chicago the gloomy patches of clouds rolled away and the sun broke through the rifts enveloping all the pageant into a mellow flood of light," wrote one observer. "At every street and by-way, as the train rolled through the suburbs of the city, the crowd of expectant people increased, the men standing with heads uncovered."

In the distance there was the faint sound of tolling bells and guns firing a tribute, but in the sea of the crowd there was stark silence.

At the Soldiers' Home of Fairview stood a brave group of "formerly maimed" veterans of the war, along with troops on duty at Camp Douglas. Together, according to one bystander, "they gave the soldier's salute and stood reverently as, with slackened speed, the train moved cityward. The Soldiers' Home was beautifully decorated."

Next, the train arrived at a temporary station near Park Row, about one mile north of the true Union Depot. It halted at point just opposite of Park Place—a short street then running directly from the lake shore one block west to Michigan Avenue.

Lincoln Funeral hearse car under guard on the old tracks of the Illinois Central Railroad by Lake Michigan during its Chicago stop in May of 1865. *Prints and Photographs Division, Library of Congress.*

A giant funeral arch stood strikingly in the air at Park Place. It was entirely made of wood, "in the Gothic style of architecture." The central arch was 30 feet tall and 24 feet wide. There were two side arches each 30 feet tall and eight feet wide. Over the three arches and their columns stretched into the Chicago sky more than 40 feet. The overall width was more than 50 feet.

Draped horse-drawn hearse bearing the coffin of President Lincoln passes an ornamental arch at 12th Street in Chicago. At the center is the word "Lincoln," partly obscured by the head of a military guard. *Prints and Photographs Division, Library of Congress.*

Above the triple structure were 50 American flags, "with mourning drapery interwoven." Busts and portraits of President Lincoln had been placed "conspicuously" upon the massive arches as well.

Furthermore, near the top of the central arch stood two American eagle figures One of the eagles had its wings folded at the front, "as if at rest." The other eagle had its wings extended, "as if in the act of taking flight."

All three of the arches had inscriptions on each front. Among them were:

"Our Union; cemented in patriot blood shall stand forever."

"An honest man is the noblest work of God."

"The poor man's champion; the people mourn him."

"We honor him dead, who honored us while living."

"Faithful to right, a martyr to justice."

Then there was the remarkable dais.

The dais was covered with black velvet and decorated with silver fringe and silver stars. Black velvet hung in festoons to all sides of it nearly to the ground.

"It was sufficiently elevated for those at a distance to view it over the heads of the surrounding multitude," commented an observer. The area immediately around the dais was large enough to provide standing room for thousands of people, and it did. Long before the train had arrived the area was a vast tide of human features.

"Every window was filled with faces, and every doorstep and piazza was filled with human beings," wrote one impressed correspondent, "while every tree along the route was eagerly climbed by adventurous juveniles. The roofs of the houses too were covered. Every place that could be any possibility of being used as seeing room was appropriated."

The whole of Lake Park extending to the east of Michigan Avenue was one vast population. The mass of spectators spread out even to the water's edge.

There were, by several estimates, thousands of school children from both public and private schools immediately in front of the general crowds.

"Next were the immobile spectators. Farther along the line, deep down the avenue as the eye could reach, extended the throng, the draped regalia of the different societies showing conspicuously, and setting against a solid background of marble palaces all fringed in mourning, and many of them elaborately decorated."

Behind all that was the "still, clear surface" of mighty Lake Michigan. *The Chicago Tribune* later described it as, "long ruffled by storm, suddenly calmed from their angry roar in solemn silence, as if they, too, felt that silence was an impressive necessity of the mournful occasion."

It was almost time to begin the grand procession downtown.

A group of high school girls, dressed in white uniforms that were banded with black crepe, walked silently around the funeral bier, depositing generous selections of fresh flowers upon the coffin.

Finally, the coffin was carried to the awaiting hearse and the funeral cortege began its slow yet purposeful procession out of Park Place and onto Michigan Avenue.

First came the Chicago Police Department, and then came the band playing the Lincoln Requiem. Next in line came Chief Marshall of the procession, Colonel R.M. Hough, along with Major General John Hooker. They were immediately followed by other high-ranking military officers and the Military Band.

Behind the group were the 400 men of the Eighth Veteran Reserve Corps under the command of Lieutenant Colonel Edward Skinner. The troops marched with their firearms in reverse position. Behind them was another military band followed by the 15th Regiment Reserve Corps, another group 400 strong with firearms in reverse position. The reserves were under the command of Lieutenant Colonel Martin Flood.

Further back were the designated pall bearers, another military escort, and the originally appointed Guard of Honor. Carriages followed bearing relatives and friends of the President and other dignitaries,

A campaign poster from the 1860 of Abraham Lincoln and Hannibal Hamlin for the Republican party in the presidential election. *Skinner, Inc.*

including Judge David Davis of the United States Supreme Court.

Members of U.S. Congress now followed. Next were a group of governors, including Governor Oliver Morton of Indiana, W.H. Wallace of Idaho territory, and Governor William Pickering of Washington territory. Behind them were members of the press and Chicago's Committee of One Hundred.

Much of the rest of the enormous procession was separated into five grand divisions, each under a marshal with a staff of aides. Notable groups including the Board of Trade, Mercantile Association, Free Masons (about 1,000 members), Odd Fellows (also about 1,000 members), students of Chicago University, both the Holland Society and the Belgian Society, "and societies belonging to citizens from other European countries." There was also what was reported as about 400 "colored citizens" in one of the procession divisions.

All together it was estimated that 37,000 persons participated in the actual funeral procession itself. It was a scant number considering those who stood and witnessed it.

The Chicago Tribune deemed it "safe to say that, including strangers and citizens who came upon the streets bordering the route of procession, there were not far from 120,000 souls who participated in and witnessed the sad ceremonies."

The thousands in the somber procession had moved west from Park Place to Michigan Avenue, then north on Michigan Avenue to Lake Street, then west on Lake Street to Clark Street, then south on Clark Street to the east side of the Court House Square.

Generally the route had been guarded on either side by strong ropes which had

Lincoln funeral procession as it proceeds to the courthouse in Chicago, May 1, 1865. Most of the downtown buildings are draped in mourning. *Prints and Photographs Division, Library of Congress.*

been stretched along the outer edge of the sidewalks. Meanwhile as the procession fully jammed the streets along the route, so were the sidewalks equally jammed with spectators.

"It was just a wilderness of banners and flags," reported one newspaper correspondent at the astonishing scene, "with their prairie of mottoes and inscriptions."

Along the way, on either side of the route, "were among the finest buildings of their kind in the world, and their owners had been lavish in the expenditure of money draping them with mourning insignia and otherwise decorating them."

The mansion of Lieutenant Governor William Bross was said to be beautifully draped with black and white crepe, interwoven with the national colors. The home of Honorable J. Y. Scammon bore on its front a bust of Lincoln, surrounded with wreaths of flowers, and surmounted by a black cherub. The Anchor of Hope was "beautifully arranged among the mourning drapery."

The residence of a leading Bishop of the Roman Catholic Church displayed national flags of Ireland and America intertwined. There were also many homes with inscription signs such as these:

"Bear him gently to his rest."

"Freedom's noblest sacrifice."

"Nations swell thy funeral cry."

"To Union may our heartfelt call And brotherly love attune us all."

"Young, old, high and low, The same devotion show."

"We loved him much, but now we love him more."

"Look how honor glorifies the dead. And over the coffin man planteth hope."

"Thousands and tens of thousands of dollars were expended in decorating the buildings with mourning drapery," one journalist noted.

The Chicago Fire Department took pride in following the procession.

Interestingly, among the military who paraded that memorable day in Chicago was a full regiment of infantry composed of men who had initially served in the Confederate States of America army. After taking the oath of allegiance to the United States while being held in various prisoner of war camps, including Camp Douglas in Chicago, they were briefly recruited into U.S. government service.

Elsewhere in the city, also from Camp Douglas, were soldiers of the 24th Ohio Battery. One detachment served the firing guns at Park Place, while the remainder acted as mounted guards in various parts of the line of march.

Regarding the whole event the *Chicago Tribune* observed: "The procession was a solemn tribute to his memorial and evinced the devotion with which all classes looked upon Mr. Lincoln. Its composition was varied, and embraced all nationalities, all creeds, and all sects. Bronzed war-worn and gray-bearded heroes of the army and navy, veteran soldiers incapacitated for active service by honorable wounds; governors of States, and grave, thoughtful-faced counselors of the nation; metropolitan officials irrespective of partisan differences; the children of the schools by the thousands, unconsciously participating in a ceremony which in after years will be their most precious recollection..."

As planned the remains of President Lincoln and the leading part of the procession arrived at the Cook County Court House about 15 minutes before 1 p.m. Just above the entryway was this inscription: "Illinois clasps to her bosom her slain and glorified son."

A "glorious" catafalque had been erected in the center of the Court House rotunda, directly beneath the towering dome. The coffin, extracted from the hearse and borne by guards, was placed on the dais within the catafalque. Afterwards the entire procession slowly passed through the rotunda in the

PRESIDENT LINCOLN'S FUNERAL—PROCESSION IN CHICAGO, ILLINOIS.
[PHOTOGRAPHED BY ATSCHULET, CHICAGO.]

Panorama of the scene in downtown Chicago as President Lincoln's funeral procession moves along. This view is an actual page from *Harper's Weekly*, published some time after the ceremony on May 27, 1865. *Owner's collection.*

order observed in the procession's marching through the streets. Oddly, this ceremony was completed well before the coffin was actually opened.

It had taken several hours for the entire somber process. It was now about 5 p.m.

The embalmers and assistants then spent a short amount of time refreshing the remains, and the long-waiting masses of people were finally admitted to view the open coffin of President Lincoln.

Immediately the area was flooded with people.

"The arrangements for exhibiting the body were excellent and the visitors passed through the rotunda without confusion," wrote one observer. Those who hurriedly passed by apparently had only time to glance at the "revered remains" as they were moved along at the remarkable rate of about 7,000 an hour.

As the day stretched into evening various songs and hymns were performed both as solos and as concerted pieces. Among them on this occasion were, "Lord, I Yield My Spirit.'" and the choral, "Happy And Blest." It included the words, "Farewell, father, friend and guardian," by L.M. Dawn, and music by George F. Root. Root was a noted composer then living in Chicago, working for a publishing house there. He also wrote music relating to Lincoln's death, and eventually the music for the well-known, "Jesus Loves the Little Children."

A drizzling rain was back again around 9 p.m., but the long and steady lines of mourners continued outside.

"And yet it was long after midnight before there was much diminution in the crowds which sought to get a last look at the dead President, " commented an observer. "They surged through the rotunda as enduring and constant as a river."

At midnight in the rotunda several hundred voices chanted a requiem in German. It was described as providing a "chilling effect."

As the day ended it was estimated that some 40,000 people—in addition to those directly from the procession—had passed the coffin of President Lincoln.

Earlier General Benjamin Sweet, commander of the prisoner of war prison at Camp Douglas, appointed an alternative guard of honor from the Veteran Reserve Corps. Sweet had been seriously wounded during the Battle of Perrysville and had lost the use of his right arm. Sweet is also credited with uncovering a plot by Confederate spies to liberate some of the prisoners at Camp Douglas shortly before the 1864 Presidential election. In December of that same year, President Lincoln promoted Sweet to the rank of brevet brigadier general. Just months before the funeral train ran, the promotion had been confirmed by the U.S. Senate.

Camp Douglas was not only a place for prisoners of war. Under Sweet, it was also a training and detention camp for Union soldiers. For a time it housed those Union soldiers who had been part of a prisoner exchange with Confederate forces. Historians often cite the deplorable conditions of the actual prisoner of war area and a very high death rate of prisoners kept there. At one time, more than 26,000 Confederate prisoners had been confined at Camp Douglas.

As it turns out, General Sweet's appointments at the Lincoln rites "to relieve those who had acted in that capacity from Washington," was unnecessary. A group of 50 Illinois veterans, who had formerly served in the Army and Navy, had already volunteered their services through General Julius White to act as a temporary Honor Guard while the remains were in Chicago. General Townsend had accepted the offer.

Those now detailed to guard the remains in the rotunda of the court house included Colonel Edward Daniels, Colonel Hasbrouc Davis, Lieutenant Colonel Arthur C. Ducat, and Captain R. L. Law of the United States Navy. Each officer had nine officers under him for alternating shifts.

At the end of a long day some observers also cited Colonel Hough, who had indeed been leading the procession as Chief Marshal, for his handling of 40,000 men in the crowded streets of a city like Chicago. "The skill and judgment of Colonel Hough in the procession was equal to managing twice the number in open ground," declared one correspondent, "and won the praise of all military men participated in the epic procession."

And more praise.

Of the overall operation in Chicago regarding President Lincoln's funeral procession, one eye-witness compared it to the funerals of England's royalty:

"I have seen three deceased Kings of England lying in state, but never have I witnessed a demonstration so vast in its proportions, so unanimous and spontaneous, as that which has been evoked by the arrival in the city of the remains of the fallen President."

By the evening of Tuesday, May 2, it was estimated by some that the number of mourners filing past the casket in the Court House was somewhere in excess of 125,000. There were different points of view as to the condition of the body, which was being subject to more and more "attention and preparation" by embalmers. Some newspapers reported the president's features appeared calm as if in a gentle sleep. However, still other journalistic accounts noted that the body's discoloration and deterioration was distressing to some viewers.

Both accounts could possibly have been correct depending on how much refinement had been done immediately before a particular group of mourners might have passed the remains.

At any rate, the viewing ended at around 8 p.m. on Tuesday as the mammoth doors of the Court House were closed, "even with a throng still pouring in." By 8:30 p.m. the building was cleared of everyone except the guard and the current choir. The coffin was then closed.

A few minutes later the coffin was carefully carried out the entrance and down the south steps of the Court House to the awaiting funeral hearse. The Light Guard Band performed grim music as the remains were being moved in the evening's darkness.

Thousands of torches were burning brightly in the very dark night as the coffin was placed in the hearse outside the Court House.

An immense procession was already formed there and it extended out some distance from the building. Around 8:45 p.m. it began moving slowing to the time and tune of numerous bands providing music.

Now the evening route was west on Washington Street to Market Street, south on Market Street to Madison Street, west on Madison by the Madison Street bridge to Canal Street on the west side, then south on Canal Street to the awaiting train depot of the Chicago, Alton & St. Louis Railroad.

At the site, while additional preparations were underway, a choir there continued to sing funeral songs and hymns, and the 25 Sergeants of the Veteran Reserve Corps stood around the funeral hearse with drawn swords.

At 9:30 p.m. the funeral cortege moved slowly away from the depot to the strains of an additional funeral march by the band, "while the bells of the city tolled a solemn farewell to all that was mortal of Abraham Lincoln."

The *Chicago Times* issue of May 3, reflecting back on the two previous days of the Lincoln Funeral Train and the rites conducted in that city, noted:

"The bitterness of his political opponents in life, vied with his warmest adherents in speaking words of appreciation and esteem. Some of the most touching and characteristic reminiscences of his personal traits, and of his private deeds, were contributed with tearful eye and broken voice by his former opponents.

"All jointed heartily and liberally in preparation for the ceremonies, which yesterday (Tuesday, May 2) and the day before were to put the seal of the people's approbation on his character and acts in the eye of the world. If men no longer went about their preparations with heavy and overburdened hearts, they did so with subdued and kindly ones.

"All was done with a tenderness more touching than the most uncontrollable passion of grief could be. When the sacred remains were brought through the streets and deposited in the keep of the people of the city, there were no downcast countenances, but none that were not sad and pitiful.

"There were no loud voices in the unnumbered throngs. Men expressed themselves in subdued tones, and often nothing could be heard but the indescribable murmur of tens of thousands of voices, modulated to a whisper, and careful tread of countless feet on the damp pavements of the streets.

"It was an entire population of a great city in mourning, conscious of what was due alike to herself and the honored dead."

All praise notwithstanding, there were some concerns voiced about the cost of the two-day event.

The City Council of Chicago had paid most of the bills regarding the reception and the passage of the funeral cortege. They also covered the cost of the funeral arch at Park Place, and the decorating of the Court House. The total cost was said to be about $15,000, which would have been a sizable amount at the time.

However, one correspondent passed it off as "probably not more than a tithe of the total expenditure by citizens and associations" involved in the huge Chicago event.

As the train departed many aboard expected the remainder of the trip to be pale by comparison to what occurred in the Illinois metropolis.

"The remains had tarried so long at Chicago, while such extensive preparations were in progress in Springfield, it would not have been surprising if the people along the line had contented themselves with visiting one or the other of those places," one journalist said later, "and had omitted any demonstrations at the respective towns and cities along the route, but the love in the hearts of the people of Illinois for the memory of Abraham Lincoln would not permit them to be so easily satisfied."

And so the trip southward from Chicago to Springfield began.

At Bridgeport, "in the very suburbs of Chicago, the people had Kindled bonfires, and with torches lighted the way as the train moved slowly along." There were also "crowds of spectators" at Summit and Willow Springs stations, and in the tiny town of Lemont.

The funeral train reached Lockport at about 11:30 p.m. that evening. People holding torches lined the tracks as the train slowed. There was an immense bonfire in the background. One report observed, "The glare of light revealed the mourning drapery on almost every building, and many mottoes expressive of the feelings of the people."

Then this comment was added: "None elicited more sympathetic feeling than the simple words: 'Come Home.'"

It was midnight and raining when the train arrived at Joliet.

At least 12,000 people—men, women, and children—were assembled in the continuing cold drizzle that hovered over the depot. A very large arch spanned the track and it was decorated profusely with flags, evergreens, and many slogan signs. One banner proclaimed, "Champion, defender and martyr of liberty."

Lincoln hearse car is shown on a rail siding in Chicago after being prepared for the final journey to Springfield, Illinois. *Prints and Photographs Division, Library of Congress.*

Lithograph of Abraham Lincoln based on a photograph taken at Chicago in 1857. Issued initially by the Federal Bureau of National Literature and Art in Washington, D.C.

The arch itself, constructed with huge timbers, was surmounted by a figure representing the Genius of America. It was depicted as weeping.

As the train pulled away from the Joliet station, a number of men and women, on elevated platform, were singing, "There is rest for thee in heaven."

111

At Elwood and Hampton, "both very small places—the people kindled large bonfires to enable them to take a passing view of the funeral train."

It was 1 a.m. on Wednesday, May 3 when the train reached Wilmington. There were two groups waiting at the station. The first group, one of a least a hundred people, stood with torches blazing along both sides of the railway. A second group, this time around 2,000 more, stood surrounding the depot itself, which, true to form, was draped in mourning. Despite the rain, all men in the crowd were standing there with their heads uncovered.

In the next town of Gardner, all houses were draped with mourning, and illuminated. At 2 a.m. the funeral train rolled into the village of Dwight. A passenger made this observation:

"The American flag was proudly displayed, and all the buildings in view were draped in mourning. The entire population appeared to be out of doors desirous to pay respects to the memory of Lincoln. Some of the escort recognized this as the place where the Prince of Wales and his royal party were entertained."

Odell, Cayuga, Pontiac, Chenoa, and Lexington became part of the train's nighttime landscape. Towns, mourners, and bonfires slowly appeared and just as slowly disappeared from view.

By the time the train reached Towanda it was 4:30 a.m.

While noting a "large assemblage of people" there at Towanda, a passenger aboard the train also commented on its geography. "This is the highest point between Chicago and St. Louis," they wrote, "being 180 feet above the water of Lake Michigan."

Bloomington came into view at 5 a.m. The sky was at last clear and the daylight was streaming into the community along with the train. At least 5,000 people stood silently and grimly at the sight of the train.

Aboard the train a witness noted:

"There would, no doubt, have been greater demonstrations at Bloomington, but a considerable number of citizens visited Chicago, and a very large delegation had already gone, or were then on the point of going to Springfield to participate in the procession and other demonstrations of respect and mourning."

Eye-catching was a mighty banner attached to the arch over the tracks at the Bloomington depot. It read: "Go To Thy Rest."

A choir of ladies was robustly singing hymns as the train reached McLean. Such singing, according to one correspondent, "contributed to the mournful effect of the occasion, which called out almost the entire population."

Fife and muffled drum greeted the funeral train at Atlanta. It was 6 a.m. Highly visible in the large crowd were portraits of Abraham Lincoln, and mottoes such as, "Mournfully, Tenderly, Bear Him To His Grave."

ABRAHAM LINCOLN, OF ILLINOIS

Early campaign image of Abraham Lincoln of Illinois. Vintage, real photo postcard.

Next, the funeral train arrived at a town named Lincoln, at 7 a.m.

This town was named for Abraham Lincoln long before he became President of the United States. It was named for him by friends and admirers of Lincoln when he was practicing law in this part of the country.

On this very special morning, the depot was draped in mourning and ladies were dressed in white that is trimmed in black. The ladies sang a hymn as the train passed beneath an attractive arch over the track. On each column of the arch was a portrait of the deceased President. The arch offered a banner that read simply: "With Malice Toward None, With Charity For All."

There were artistic decorations everywhere in Lincoln amid the wash of evergreens and black and white drapes. The "national colors" were also frequently displayed.

At Williamsville, the houses, like so many villages of the hours and days before, were draped in mourning. There was, according to one account, "a profuse display of small flags and portraits of the late President."

On the arch at the Williamsville depot is a sign widely spanning it, which read: "He has fulfilled his mission."

Some 18 miles from Springfield the funeral train passed still another monumental arch, which was laced with both large and small American flags, mourning drapery, and a burst of evergreens. Upon the arch was a cross intertwined with black cloth; it said, in large letters, "Ours the Cross; Thine the Crown."

At Sherman Station, just eight miles from Springfield, it was noted, "many people are assembled on the road, some on horseback and some in carriages, but the larger part on foot. The number increased as the train proceeded."

This was the schedule for Illinois:

(MONDAY, MAY 1, 1865)
Chicago arrive 11 a.m.

(TUESDAY, MAY 2, 1865)
Chicago depart 9:30 p.m.
Bridgeport
Summit
Willow Springs
Lemont
Lockport arrive 11:30 p.m.
Joliet arrive 12 p.m.

(WEDNESDAY, MAY 3, 1865)
Elwood
Hampton
Wilmington arrive 1 a.m.
Braidwood
Braceville
Gardner
Dwight arrive 2 a.m.
Odell
Cayuga
Pontiac
Chenoa
Lexington
Normal (Towanda) arrive 4:30 a.m.
Bloomington arrive 5 a.m.
Shirley (Funk's Grove)
McClean
Atlanta arrive 6 a.m.
Lincoln arrive 7 a.m.
Elkhart
Williamsville
Clinton
Kenny
Chestnut
Mt. Pulaski
Lake Ford
Cornland
Buffalo Hart
Barclay
Clinton
Springfield arrive 9 a.m.

[Handwritten letter]

On this general subject, I respectfully refer Mr. Browne to the Secretaries of War and Navy for conference and consultation.

I have a single idea of my own about harbor defences. It is a Steam-ram, built so as to sacrifice nearly all capacity for carrying, to those those of speed and strength, so as to be able to split any vessel having hollow enough in her to carry supplies for a voyage of any distance. Such ram, of course could not herself carry supplies for a voyage of considerable distance; and her business would be to guard a particular harbor, as a Bull-dog guards his master's door

A. Lincoln

April 4, 1863.

President Abraham Lincoln's hand-written letter to Governor John Andrew of Massachusetts concerning his option for the defense of Boston Harbor, together with Governor Andrew's original letter of request. In the Lincoln reply the President suggests a Steam-ram adding, "such ram, of course, could not herself carry supplies for a voyage of considerable distance; and her business would be to guard a particular harbor, as a Bull-dog guards his master's door." The letter is dated April 4, 1863. *Skinner, Inc.*, estimated $30,000–$50,000.

Journey's End

(Springfield, Illinois)

And yet more than the political leader he was the popular townsman and good neighbor at his home in Springfield. Springfield then, his proper burial place.

—*The New-York Tribune*

It speaks to the planning of this incredible journey by rail to realize that it was all planned 12 days earlier in Washington. And yet it ended in Springfield just one hour later than originally scheduled.

The Lincoln Funeral Train arrived in Springfield at 9 a.m.

What a welcome it received.

For at least 25 hours before its arrival, trains on all other railways had been frantically hauling thousands of passengers into Springfield. By the time the Lincoln Train arrived, the community was literally teeming with visitors eager to see the train arrive at its final destination.

"The greatest anxiety was manifested by the people to be present at the reception of the remains of Abraham Lincoln," wrote one correspondent. "Long previous to the time of their arrival, crowds were collected at the Chicago & Alton Railroad, and extended along a line of the several squares (blocks) north."

CHICAGO HISTORICAL SOCIETY

LEAVING SPRINGFIELD FOR WASHINGTON, 1861   4B187-N

Enactment of President Lincoln leaving Springfield for Washington in 1861 for his inauguration, called a diorama. Lincoln is shown on the rear platform of his special train at the Great Western Railway Station. This vintage postcard was issued by the Chicago Historical Society.

Every single building in the Springfield vicinity was covered with spectators. Hundreds of people who could not find standing room near the depot, managed to somehow squeeze into areas of Fourth and Fifth streets or up to the crossing near the northern limits of the city.

It was "well known" many days beforehand that the hotels in Springfield could not come close to accommodating the teeming mass of visitors for this remarkable burial event. Many private homes were made available and a number of Masonic lodges were also made available.

"As for sleeping," quipped one observer, "there was not much of that done in Springfield on the night the remains of Abraham Lincoln were exposed to view." Added still another, "The city is so crowded that it is impossible even to procure lodging in a barroom or on a pool table."

Up to 350 workers and volunteers had been busy decorating *en masse* the State House for ten days prior to the arrival of the Lincoln train. They had labored and decorated practically day and night since learning of the President's death.

Home of Abraham Lincoln as it appeared on the day of his funeral, Springfield, Illinois. Vintage postcard, estimated $20–$30.

Fascinating photograph of people grouped around the heavily draped home of President Lincoln on May 4, 1865. It was reproduced as a postcard in 1908. Vintage postcard, estimated $40–$50.

As a result, the entire exterior of the Court House was now draped in mourning. Additionally, the interior of the rotunda and Representatives' Hall, along with the entrance to the Governor's Room and the entrances of various other state officials' offices, were decorated.

"The ladies of Springfield bore their full share in these arduous labors," noted one journalist in commenting about the splendor of it.

The decorating at the Court House had ultimately involved some 1,500 yards of black and white goods in basics alone. According to some accounts, the decorating crews had run out of black mourning material and had to finish the enormous job with white cloth, although some in the group reportedly strongly objected to the use of any white whatsoever.

Construction of the catafalque inside of the building involved copious use of black cloth; black, blue, and white silk and crepe; plus great numbers of silver stars, along with silver lace and fringe.

Specifically, the canopy of the catafalque had been made of velvet, further enhanced with satin and silver fringe. It had been lined on the underside with blue silk, and studded with silver stars. Overall, the construction required 300 yards of velvet and mourning goods, plus another 300 yards of silver lace and fringe.

For further embellishment, the Court House was laced with 200 vases of natural flowers in full bloom that "emitted their fragrance throughout the edifice." Most of the flowers had been generously furnished without cost by local Springfield horticulturist Michael Doyle.

The whole thing, to say the least, was big news.

Proclaimed the *Illinois State Journal* right there in Springfield:

"Today all that is mortal of Abraham Lincoln comes back to us to be deposited among a people with whom he hoped, his work being done, to spend the evening of his days."

The mighty *New-York Tribune* took a more worldly approach in its editions:

"Springfield has been the home of Abraham Lincoln for 25 years. With his companionable nature and open heart it followed that he was the personal acquaintance and friend of all men, women and children in the city, and in all the region around about.

This is a large format silver albumen print of Abraham Lincoln taken at Lincoln's home in Springfield in June of 1860 by Alexander Hesler. It was later printed by George Ayers of Philadelphia. The print is approximately 8 and one half inches by 6 and one half inches. *Skinner, Inc.*, estimated $3,000–$4,000.

"Besides, Springfield was the political center of the State, and during 20 years Abraham Lincoln was an acknowledged State leader of a political party. That part, or the one that sprang from it, was finally successful, and rewarded him not merely with State honors, but the headship of the nation.

"Such men as E.D. Baker, Lyman Trumbull, Richard Yates, S. T. Logan, David Davies, Owen Lovejoy, E. B. Washburne, William H. Bissell, R.J. Oglesby, J.N. Arnold, and John Wentworth—all these conceded his right to leadership, and cheerfully rallied beneath his standard.

"And yet more than the political leader, he was the popular townsman and good neighbor at his home in Springfield. Springfield, then, is his proper burial place."

When the pilot train made its appearance shortly before 9 a.m., guns had already been firing in the distance by a section of Battery K, Second Missouri Light Artillery.

"The ten minutes between its (pilot train) arrival and that of the actual funeral train were occupied by General John Cook," according to one witness, "in bringing to their proper places the committee of reception, members of several delegations, the military and civil societies."

Cook was a native of Illinois and had initially served as a Colonel in the 7th Illinois Volunteer Regiment. He commanded the 3rd Brigade during the Battle of Fort Donelson. During his distinguished war career he was promoted to the rank of brigadier general of the Volunteers, and eventually rose to commander of the Sixth Division in the Army of Tennessee. At the time of the funeral train's arrival, General Cook was acting as commander of the military District of Illinois. Earlier he had fought against the Sioux Nation in campaigns in the Great West.

As soon as the funeral train arrived at the Springfield depot, the coffin bearing President Lincoln was transferred to a beautifully constructed hearse. The hearse had

been provided especially for the occasion by the Lynch & Arnot Company of St. Louis through the mayor of St. Louis. The grand hearse had been built in the city of Philadelphia, at a then enormous cost of $6,000, "and was larger than the ordinary size."

Oddly, the remarkable hearse had been used once before, and after its offer to the officials of Springfield, it was additionally ornamented with the silver plate engraving of the initials "A. L." The area around the initials was then surrounded with a silver wreath, two inverted torches, and 36 silver stars representing the States of the Union.

The stunning hearse was drawn by six radiant black horses draped in mourning, wearing plumes on their crests. The horses also belonged to the Lynch and Arnot firm, and were actually driven by A. Arnot himself without the aid of grooms.

Old Bob, the legendary old horse owed by President Lincoln, is shown in front of the heavily decorated Lincoln home in Springfield, Illinois. This photograph was taken shortly before the Lincoln Funeral Train arrived. *Prints and Photographs Division, Library of Congress.*

Grainy old photograph depicts Lincoln's horse Old Bob decorated for funeral rites with his trainer. *Prints and Photographs Division, Library of Congress.*

After all were in readiness, the elaborate procession from the train depot to the Court House was ready to begin.

General Cook and his aides took the lead as a hushed throng of thousands watched from every possible angle.

Next came the 146th Regiment of the Illinois Volunteer Infantry under the command of Colonel H. H. Deane. Also acting as military escort for the movement was Captain William Chase and one company of the 46th Regiment of the Wisconsin Volunteer Infantry, and Lieutenant E. Coruelius with Company E of the Veteran Reserve Corps.

Close behind them was the military band in full and robust function.

Immediately behind the military band were Major General Joseph Hooker and his staff of officers. Behind the general were the pallbearers and Guard of Honor, which had been with the remains since the beginning of the journey.

Next were various high-ranking military officers, members of the Illinois State Legislature, Governors of different states, a delegation from Kentucky, and then the Chicago Committee of One Hundred. Later the Committee of One Hundred, less a few members whose "business engagements prevented" them from attending, would assemble at Lincoln's residence for photographs. The photographer was an artist from Chicago who accompanied the group to Springfield for the purpose of taking views of the State House, the rites at Oak Ridge, and similar surroundings.

"Strangers who were in the city, on this occasion for the first time, almost invariably visited the former residence of President Lincoln, at the north east corner of Eighth and Jackson streets," wrote one journalist. "It was elaborately and tastefully decorated with the national colors and insignia of sorrow."

They likely also visited the Governor's Mansion, which was also heavily decorated, as was the military headquarters of General Cook and General George Oakes, and a vast number of other Springfield buildings.

Later it would be revealed that of the $20,000 appropriated by the City Council of Springfield for the funeral, less than $15,000 was actually used. Part of that amount was for the construction of a temporary vault, paying railroad charges on some carriages from Jacksonville, Florida, and has previously been noted the hearse from St. Louis. There were also the expenses of the musicians and the orator later at the cemetery services.

However, the largest portion of the whole amount was spent in decorating the State House building. Even so a great deal more was spent by private businesses and individuals because the whole city was draped for the sobering event, often "as richly decorated as public buildings."

Further behind the procession were the Springfield Committee of Reception, judges of various courts, clergy, and the officers of the Army and Navy either presently in service or honorably discharged.

Finally, there were various civic groups and the general population of citizens at the distant rear of a very long procession.

The procession moved from the depot on east Jefferson Street to Fifth Street, south on Fifth Street to Monroe Street, east on Monroe Street to Sixth, and north on Sixth Street to the State House Square, entering through the east gate, and then by the north door into the State House to the Representatives'

THE FATHER

PRESIDENT LINCOLN'S FUNERAL—CATAFALQUE IN THE CITY [

[SKETCHED BY W. WAUD.]

This sketch by William Waud is an actual clipping from the original May 1865 edition of *Harper's Weekly*. The scene is Lincoln's funeral catafalque there in city hall at Springfield, Illinois. *Author's collection*.

INGFIELD, ILLINOIS.

Guards are standing along the walkway as mourners move toward the north door of the Illinois statehouse in Springfield, Illinois. Inside they viewed the remains of President Lincoln. *Prints and Photographs Division, Library of Congress.*

Hall in the west end of the building, on the second story.

This was the place where Lincoln had given has famous "House Divided" speech, and this would be the location where an estimated 75,000 people would look upon him for the last time.

"The cortege, more solemn than any had gone before, reaches the State House," reported the *New-York Tribune*, "where he went to speak face to face to his neighbors—where at this hour those neighbors press to behold his face locked in death."

Strong arms placed the coffin on a dais, "within a magnificent catafalque prepared for the occasion."

At a few minutes passed 10 a.m. the doors were opened and the vast crowd already waiting outside began to quietly file into the hall to view the remains. Mourners entered the Capitol at the north door, ascended the stairway in the rotunda and entered the Representatives' Hall at the north. Silently they passed by the catafalque, and moved out at the south door, then through the door at the stairway and made their exit from the Capitol at the south side.

"No human voices were heard except in subdued tones; but the tramp, tramp of busy feet, as men and women filed through the

State House; up one flight of stairs, through the hall, and down another stairway, testified the love and veneration for Abraham Lincoln in the hearts of old friends and neighbors," said one chronicle.

Yet even with the quiet of visitors, there was music in the air.

A group of 30 singers, accompanied by Leburn's Washington Band of 20 performers from St. Louis, assembled on the steps outside of the Court House. Under the direction of Professor Ludwig Meissner, they impassionedly sang: "Peace, Troubled Soul."

In the midst of it all, the *New-York Tribune* could not refrain from expressing still more concern about the condition of the body at this point, despite noting the eloquence of the decorum.

"All night they will pass by with eyes searching through tears for resemblances and recognition of the features they knew so well. Many will not know the poor, chilled, shrunken features for his, for the beautiful soul that transfigured them into all loveliness no longer illumines the bit of clay—aye, but it shines at the Right Hand!"

On the morning of Thursday, May 4, at 10 a.m., as lines of saddened citizens and visitors waited, the coffin was closed.

As the coffin was being carried to the hearse outside, the crowd heard a chorus of hundreds of voices accompanied by a brass band. They sorrowfully sang:

"Children of the Heavenly King,

Let us journey as we sing."

Swiftly the funeral procession was formed again, this time under the direct supervision of General Hooker acting as marshal-in-chief.

The first division of the procession consisted entirely of infantry, cavalry, and artillery. Next came a division of various officers and enlisted men in both the Army and Navy.

Other divisions followed the growing formation, including Old Bob, the aging horse once ridden by Lincoln during his law practice and during political campaigns. The horse, now 16 years old, was covered with black cloth and trimmed with silver fringe. It was led by two grooms.

Not far behind were the pallbearers. They included: Jesse K. Dubois, S.T. Logan, Gustavus Koerner, James L. Lamb, S. H. Treat, Colonel John Williams, Erastus Wright, J.N. Brown, Jacob Bunn, Elijah Iles, and John T. Stuart.

They were smartly followed by the familiar Guard of Honor riding in carriages and family and friends also in carriages. There were still more military units closely following them, and then an "army" of legislators.

Yet another somber unit was composed of "Christian, Sanitary and other kindred Commissions, Aid Societies, and delegations from universities, colleges, and other institutions of learning."

For a place like Springfield, this whole thing was indeed awesome.

"Never before was there so large a military and civic display in Springfield," wrote one correspondent. "There were immense crowds of people in the immediate vicinity of the Capitol to see the procession as it passed, and the people for several miles occupied the side-ways."

Still the numbers of those participating in this final procession continued.

Free Masons, Odd Fellows, firemen, and assorted fraternities came marching along. African-Americans were noticeably the last group in the procession. They were just behind what was described as, "citizens generally, and all who had not been assigned to some other place in the procession."

The long and winding parade of those paying a last tribute now extended into the thousands. They would ultimately march about a mile and a half in total from their start at the Court House Square.

That morning the *Illinois State Journal* had declared:

"Today we lay him reverently to rest, amid the scenes he loved so well. Millions will drop a tear to his memory, and future generations will make pilgrimages to his tomb. Peace to his ashes."

This sweeping view of President Abraham Lincoln's funeral rites and burial at Oak Ridge just outside of Springfield, Illinois is a sketch by journalist/artist William Waud. Shown here is an original page from the May 27, 1865 issue of *Harper's Weekly*. *Author's collection.*

The procession moved east on Washington Street to Eighth, south on Eighth—passing the Lincoln residence at the corner of Jackson and Eighth—to Cook Street, then west on Cook to Fourth, then north on Fourth—passing the Governor's Mansion—to Union Street, west on Union to Third Street, north on Third to the eastern entrance of majestic Oak Ridge Cemetery.

"On arriving at the cemetery, the remains were carefully and gently placed in the receiving tomb," according one report at the scene. "Following that the choir sang softly as the many silently gathered around the burial location."

The coffin now rested on a marble slab. Next to the coffin and body of Lincoln was a smaller coffin containing the body of young Willie Lincoln. They are surrounded by an especially built vault and tomb.

Coffins of President Abraham Lincoln and son William "Willie" Lincoln are side by side during entombment at Oak Ridge Cemetery in May of 1865. William died while the family was living in the White House. President Lincoln and Mrs. Lincoln were the only First Family to undergo the death of a child while living there. Earlier a son, Edward, died while they were living in Springfield. *Prints and Photographs Division, Library of Congress.*

On the outside the tomb has been constructed of limestone mined from nearby Joliet, Illinois. The structure has been carved from the foot of a knoll in a particularly scenic part of the cemetery grounds, which also contains a forest of trees of all varieties. The vault itself stands 15 feet high and is about the same in width, with semi-circular wings of bricks projecting from the sides.

The interior walls are covered with black velvet, and it is dotted with evergreens. In the center of the velvet is a foundation of brick, capped with the marble slab upon which the President's coffin has been placed.

As a softer touch, the vault is completely trimmed with evergreens.

On the left of the decorated Lincoln vault was a platform for those invited for singing as well as an instrumental band. Together they

This is reported to be the first oil portrait of Abraham Lincoln, painted by Thomas Hicks in June of 1860 at Springfield, Illinois. The portrait is in the collection of the Chicago Historical Society, and is reproduced on this 20th century postcard.

President Lincoln's Casket inside his Monument at Oak Ridge Cemetery, Springfield, Ill.

COPYRIGHTED BY C. J. RESLER, TAYLORVILLE, ILL.

Early 1900s view of President Lincoln's "casket inside his monument at Oak Ridge Cemetery." Vintage postcard, estimated $15–$25.

performed various selections in sorrowful tones, including a burial hymn.

On the right of the vault was a speaker's stand appropriately draped with cloth material of mourning. Thousands of people were assembled at the cemetery as the services began. Their numbers flooded over the grounds and also spilled out into the green hills that surrounded the cemetery. "The landscape was beautiful," commented one witness, "in the light of an unclouded sun."

The ceremonies alternated from various orations to the singing of the choir and reading of various Scriptures. At one point, Reverend Dr. David Simpson, Bishop of the Methodist Episcopal Church, addressed the audience. Rev. Simpson reviewed the life of Lincoln, and then added:

This real photo postcard features the Lincoln Monument at Springfield decades after the original Lincoln funeral rites.

"Far more eyes have gazed upon the face of the departed than ever looked upon the face of any other departed man. More eyes have looked upon the process for sixteen hundred miles and more, by night and day, by sunlight, dawn, twilight, and by torchlight, than ever before watched the progress of a procession."

Rev. Simpson paused, and further added:

"Nor is this mourning confined to any one class, or any district or country. Men of all political parties and of all religious creeds have united in paying this mournful tribute. The archbishop of the Roman Catholic Church in New York and a Protestant minister walked side by side in the sad procession. A Jewish Rabbi performed part of the solemn services."

When the Bishop's message was concluded, one in attendance later wrote, "It was in the highest degree solemn, eloquent, and patriotic, and portions of it were applauded."

The closing was left to Dr. P. D. Gurley, who was presented as the president's own personal minister. He addressed the bereaved attending, and then offered a final prayer. Afterwards, the choir sang a hymn that Dr. Gurley had composed himself. The final stanza of it was as follows:

"O, God, before whom we, in tears,
Our fallen chief deplore
Grant that the cause for which he died,
May live forever more."

And then it was over.

The funeral procession was steadfastly re-formed and more or less returned from the outskirts of Springfield.

Throngs and throngs of people who had flocked to the burial site and all remaining areas nearby simply departed nearly as quietly and as drearily as they had assembled earlier in the day.

One of the many journalists at the scene described the closing of services and the departing of the public thusly, "when the vast multitude melted away and sought the railroad depots, from which the trains bore them to their homes in all parts of the nation—east, west, north and south. Thus ended the most grand and sublime funeral pageant the world had ever seen."

For all of its grandness and its phenomenal planning, the journey of the Lincoln Funeral Train was universally touching.

Millions of everyday Americans, without prompting or urging from any source, simply showed up to pay their respects. They offered somber respect for that President and that train as it passed through their community—night or day, rain or shine, stopping for full rites or simply rumbling through the village.

It was as authentic as it was spontaneous.

For Americans living in the midst of the 19th century it was their mutual witnessing of history.

Hand-written letter from Abraham Lincoln in Springfield, Illinois sent to the Honorable Julius Rockwell. It was concerning the signing of a blank bond to his son Robert, attending Harvard University. It reads in part, "My son, who has entered Harvard University, sends you the enclosed blank bond, which, with the head note, explains itself." Enclosed with it was a thank you note signed by Robert T. Lincoln. *Skinner, Inc.* estimated $15,000–$20,000.

Check signed by Abraham Lincoln, drawn from the Springfield Marine & Fire Insurance Company, and made payable to Smith Wickersham & Company. The amount was $153.46 and the date was March 21, 1860. Historical accounts say Lincoln was standing in front of this shop when he received the news of his nomination as the Republican party candidate. *Skinner, Inc.*, estimated $10,000–$12,000.

Real photo postcard depicts the home of President Lincoln in Springfield, Illinois after some restoration.

Abraham Lincoln and Mary Todd Lincoln depicted next to their home in Springfield, Illinois. Ultimately both were buried in Oak Ridge Cemetery. Vintage postcard, estimated $10–$14.

Goodbye

(Lincoln's Funeral Car)

"If God had not loved the common people,
He would not have made so many of them."

—Abraham Lincoln

Most people would expect the Lincoln Funeral Car—perhaps the most historic rail car in American history—to be housed forever in some distinguished and enduring museum. It is not so.

In fact, the converted Presidential car that became a Presidential hearse on wheels, and drew millions to stand alongside countless of miles of railroad track in awe and sorrow, no longer exists.

Following the faithful trip from Washington to Springfield, the elaborately decorated hearse rail car was never used again by the federal government. In 1866, with the Civil War ended and the military-controlled railroad system being returned to civilian control in the United States, there was no official use for it.

Perhaps at that point some Congressional committee or some enterprising group

The hearse car of President Abraham Lincoln as it stood at a siding in Chicago, Illinois. The car had exceptional wheels that could accommodate any gauge (width) railroad track. *Prints and Photographs Division, Library of Congress.*

The Lincoln Funeral Car image offered as a souvenir of the 42nd National Encampment of the Grand Army of the Republic. Real photo postcard, estimated $10–$20.

of private citizens could have spoken up and even financed the cost to save it for prosperity. Thus far no record has been found of any such sustained and successful effort.

Little more than a year after President Lincoln's burial, the U.S. government sold the hearse car, which had logged less than 1,700 miles, to the Union Pacific Railroad for the price of $6,800.

Now it became the personal car of railroad builder and transportation legend Thomas C. Durant. Durant was so immortal in railroad lore that he was depicted nearly a century and a half later in the AMC television series *Hell On Wheels* by actor Colm Meaney. True to form Durant was featured in the TV series as a key figure in overseeing the construction of Union Pacific's part of the transcontinental railroad.

Oddly, Durant initially had a career in medicine. He held a degree from a medical college and even once taught surgery. However, he left a budding medical career to join a family-owned grain exporting company. As the story goes, his interest in expanding inland transportation routes led to his further involvement in the railroad industry starting first with the Chicago and Rock Island Railroad.

While in the railroad transportation business, one of his major accomplishments was the design and construction of a wooden

railroad bridge. When completed it spanned the Mississippi River for the Mississippi and Missouri Railroad (M & M).

Durant made most of his fortune acting as the chief financier of the Credit Mobilier of America, which funded railroad construction in general and the Union Pacific in particular. Later Durant reportedly lost much of his wealth in the economic depression of 1873.

It is likely that Durant was woefully short of funds when he sold the Lincoln hearse car to the Colorado Central Railroad for $3,000 the following year—a considerable loss from his initial investment.

The CCR certainly had no lofty plans for the car. In fact, they stripped it of all its elaborate trappings and decorations, and put it to use as part of the regular passenger service on the Colorado line.

They also made one other major change.

The United States had finally adopted a national standard track gauge (width) for all the railroads in the country. Until that time they had varied, often depending on the preference of a particular railroad line. Incidentally, it had been President Lincoln who had initially signed federal legislation into law during the 1860s, gradually providing a uniform standard gauge for all railroads. Consequently, the once "universal" wheels on the former hearse car, which allowed it to run virtually on any railroad line, were replaced with the now standard eight-wheel carriage.

As the years rolled on, so did the once proud Lincoln hearse car turned mere train passenger car.

In 1898, it was sold again. This time the buyer was Union Pacific, the former owner. There was an effort, however feeble, to restore the memorable car to its former glory. After some refurbishing, it was put on display at the 1904 World's Fair in St. Louis.

Barely a year later, the car was once again sold, and now the new owner was Thomas Lowry of Minneapolis, Minnesota.

The Illinois-born Lowry became an attorney, and as a young man established a law practice in Minneapolis within a few years after the end of the Civil War. Like once owner Durant, new owner Lowry made a major career change. By the middle of the 1870s, Lowry had become deeply involved in the growing operation of the Minneapolis Street Railway. Within two years he had gained controlling interest of the company, and moved toward gaining financial backing to extend the railway into undeveloped but potentially profitable territory.

Eventually the enterprising firm was merged with a nearby St. Paul railway to create an "interurban" of sorts there in the Minnesota region. In the 1890s, the company began building its own streetcars rather than to rely on other manufacturers as they had in the past. One of the first successful designs was made especially for Lowery, and included large windows at one end so the privileged passenger could see more of the scenery as the car moved along.

Similar in some ways to the original Lincoln hearse car, it was put into use only for special events and marked occasions. One such event was to transport visiting President William McKinney around Minneapolis in 1900.

At the zenith of his career, Lowry also served as president of the Soo Line Railroad. In 1905, while following his ambitious achievements, Lowry purchased the Lincoln hearse car. Optimistic plans called for again restoring the car to its original splendor and touring around the country as the last surviving part of the Lincoln Funeral Train.

Once again such a grand idea did not come to much of anything.

Some half dozen years later, on March 18, 1911, a rampaging fire destroyed ten blocks of the small community of Columbia Heights in Anoka County. The town, just northeast of the city limits of Minneapolis, included a storage shed, which in turn held the nearly unheralded Lincoln funeral car.

Remains of the once historic car were gathered up over the next few days by souvenir hunters whom had been granted such salvage permission by the owner. Whatever had survived both the fire and the crowd's gathering was declared debris to be cleared away and destroyed.

Generations later a limited number of the original hearse car furnishings are housed in the Union Pacific Collection at the Western Heritage Museum in Omaha, Nebraska.

This promotion booklet from the 1900s offers street car passengers information and viewing of The Historic Lincoln Car. It could be viewed from the street car on the outskirts of Minneapolis at Columbia Heights, but the Lincoln car was later destroyed by fire in March of 1911. (Author's collection).

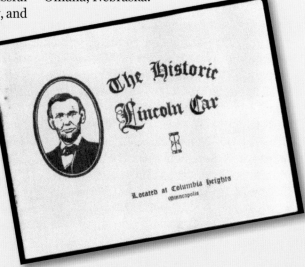

The Historic
Lincoln Car

Located at Columbia Heights
Minneapolis

(Miles)

Lithograph campaign image of "Honest Abe" Abraham Lincoln earlier in Illinois. Later it was produced by a now non-existent federal agency. *Federal Bureau of National Literature and Art.*

The journey of the Lincoln Funeral Train over much of the United States was an epic one in 1865, and even the observers at that time understood it to be historic.

Just exactly how many miles the remarkable train precisely covered is unsure. Contemporaneous sources at the time, like *Harper's Weekly* and *The New York Times,* put it somewhere between 1,500 and 1,800 miles. In later accounts it was suggested that the distance was near or exceeded 1,700 miles.

At least one 19th century account puts the number of miles at 1,662. In the book *Abraham Lincoln His Life, Public Services, Death and Great Funeral Cortege,* John C. Power offered the following:

"The annexed table will exhibit the distance traveled by the funeral train that bore the remains of Abraham Lincoln from Washington city to Springfield, Illinois. The distance is also given between the different points at which the remains were taken from the train, in compliance with the desire of people to do honor to the memory of the martyred President."

From Washington to Baltimore..40 miles

Baltimore via York to Harrisburg...84 miles

Harrisburg to Philadelphia..107 miles

Philadelphia via Trenton to New York ....87 miles

New York to Albany ....142 miles

Albany via Schnectady, Utica, Syracuse, Rochester
and Batavia to Buffalo..296 miles

Buffalo via Dunkirk and Erie to Cleveland..................................183 miles

Cleveland via Crestline and Delaware to Columbus ....138 miles

Columbus via Urbana, Piqua, Greenville, Richmond and
Knightstown to Indianapolis ....188 miles

Indianapolis via Lafayette and Michigan City to Chicago ....212 miles

Chicago via Joliet, Chenoa and Bloomington to Springfield..................185 miles

THE TOTAL MILES FOR THE FUNERAL TRAIN................................1,662 miles

Engine used for Lincoln's Funeral Train in 1865 at a railroad siding in Pennsylvania. The engine, one of many used during the nearly 1,700 mile trip, was heavily decorated with flags and mourning items. *Prints and Photographs Division, Library of Congress.*

Appendix 2

(Legislative)

Announcing the assassination death of President Abraham Lincoln to the New York General Assembly on a dreary Saturday in April must have been most difficult for Governor Ruben Fenton.

As a Congressman during the Lincoln presidency, Fenton had been a frequent White House visitor.

"My relations with President Lincoln were cordial," he once remarked.

On another occasion Fenton observed of the President, "Mr. Lincoln was keenly alive to the situation. The character and opinions of this rugged-featured and intellectually great man always enforced respect and confidence whatever the pleasantry of his manner."

Later on they became political running mates.

In seeking re-election in 1864, President Lincoln clearly needed the state of New York to hold the White House. At the time, the ever-popular Fenton was more or less drafted to run for Governor of New York.

It was mutually beneficial. Both Lincoln and Fenton carried the state of New York. Remarkably the Governor-elect ended up with 1,500 votes more totally than President

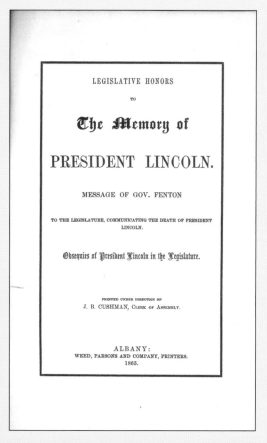

LEGISLATIVE HONORS

TO

The Memory of

PRESIDENT LINCOLN.

MESSAGE OF GOV. FENTON

TO THE LEGISLATURE, COMMUNICATING THE DEATH OF PRESIDENT LINCOLN.

Obsequies of President Lincoln in the Legislature.

PRINTED UNDER DIRECTION OF
J. B. CUSHMAN, CLERK OF ASSEMBLY.

ALBANY:
WEED, PARSONS AND COMPANY, PRINTERS.
1865.

This is the title page of Legislative Honors to The Memory of Abraham Lincoln based on a special session of the legislature of the State of New York in Albany during the month of April of 1865. *Author's collection.*

Lincoln. The *New-York Tribune* declared of it, "We believe this to be the only instance in which a Republican candidate for governor polled a heavier vote than cast for President in the same election."

The earlier very dark clouds of morning turned to increasing waves of rain by afternoon in Albany.

From the state's executive department on that April 15 Saturday came Governor Fenton's grim announcement to the State Legislature: "It becomes my painful duty to announce to the Legislature the death of Abraham Lincoln, President of the United States."

The announcement continued:

"It is with emotions of profound sorrow that I make this announcement to your honorable body. Such an event is a national calamity, and under the circumstances now attending this bereavement, the nation weeps with heightened anguish. To be deprived of his wisdom, experience and counsel, at a time when most important to return us securely to national peace, fraternity and prosperity; at a time when the gigantic war which confronted him at the threshold of his administration is about drawing to a close, and a final deliverance obtained from our civil disturbances, for which we have sacrificed so much, is a calamity that will cause the deepest sadness and gloom to millions out our land and to the friends of freedom throughout the word.

"Thus, it is the third time in our history, the Republic is subject to this trial, but it is hoped that our good cause and country, watered by a nation's tears and sanctified by its prayers, will pass safely through the ordeal to a higher life and destiny.

(Lincoln was the first president to be assassinated, but the third to die in office. President William Henry Harrison died in 1841, and President Zachary Taylor died in 1850.)

"I have also to communicate to you the sad intelligence that our noble Secretary of State, an honored and favored son of New York, William H. Seward, was likewise the victim of a tragic plot of the assassins, and now lies in an unconscious condition. May God spare his life to the nation."

—R.E. Fenton.

(Indeed, Secretary Seward was terribly injured in the assassin attack, but slowly recovered.)

Fenton had been a member of Congress for several years by the time Lincoln had been elected to the presidency. Both had been converts to the newly formed Republican Party. Fenton had originally been a Democrat and Lincoln had been a member of the Whig Party.

In 1864, Fenton was enjoying some popularity as a Congressman and was encouraged by Lincoln and many others to run for governor and engage the dashing and dramatic Governor Horatio Seymour who was confidently seeking re-election. Obviously national politics came into play as Lincoln, now up for re-election as President, would be on the same ballot.

As governor of New York, aside from his alliance with Lincoln and fierce opposition to slavery, Governor Fenton was perhaps best known for establishing a paid fire department for the city of New York. Previously the city had relied on volunteers who were sometimes accused of looting the very buildings they had previously rescued from fires.

The Governor's grim announcement of the death of President Lincoln was received at the State House in Albany. Chairman of the Senate, Charles J. Folger, and chairman of the Assembly, Thomas B. Van Buren, agreed for the two Houses to meet jointly "for such obsequies (funeral orations)."

It was also decreed that "having in mind that the funeral of the late President of the United States will probably take place on some early day in the next week, and that such day will be observed throughout the whole country as a day of solemn recognition of the tragic and awful event which now fills all thoughts..." the Houses will convene Tuesday "of next week," April 18, at 11 a.m.

At some point it was further resolved, "that the (New York) Capitol be draped in mourning, and the members and officers of both Houses wear a uniform badge of sorrow for thirty days, and that it is recommended to all citizens of this State to wear some symbol of mourning for a like period."

The New York legislature met on Tuesday and again on Wednesday of that week.

On Wednesday, April 19, as thousands thronged Pennsylvania Avenue in rainy Washington, D.C. to view the funeral procession of President Lincoln, a joint resolution was being crafted at the State House in Albany, New York. It was the work of Thomas B. Van Buren, the chairman of the Assembly, and Charles J. Folger, the chairman of the Senate.

That day Senator Folger rose to address the Senate regarding the resolution and seek its passage. The resolution read as follows:

"That the Legislature of the State of New York has received the announcement of the death of Abraham Lincoln, the late President of the United States, with emotions of profound sorrow.

"That in the character of the illustrious dead were united the patriot and statesman, whose purity of purpose and wisdom of counsel, have guided our Republic safely in its hour of greatest trial, and enshrined him in the affections of the American people.

"That this sad and afflicting event is a national bereavement, the more to be deplored that his administration, having well-nigh suppressed the gigantic rebellion in the South, promised, as its crowning act of glory, the speedy and happy pacification of the whole country.

"That the unparalleled crime, by which the nation has been deprived of the services of the chief of its own free choice, while in the active discharge of his duties, is not only revolting to the general sense of mankind, but is an outrage upon popular government, particularly deserving of the execration of the American people, and consigning to eternal infamy its perpetrators and abettors.

"That we have the highest confidence in the patriotism, good sense, virtue and religion of the American people; and we believe that, even under the greatest of calamities, they will exhibit to the world their regard for the Constitution and Laws of their country, their love of justice and order, and their firm reliance upon an all-wise and overruling Providence.

"That to God, who has been with this nation from the beginning, who, through the past four years of terrible war has guided and protected us, and who of late has so signally blessed us, do we turn in this our day of distress and humbly commit ourselves and our interests.

"That while the country mourns its loss, its sympathies are due to the bereaved family of the deceased, and that his Excellency the Governor be requested to transmit to them these resolutions, with the expression of the sincere condolence, in their great misfortune, of the people of this State.

"That to the Honorable William H. Seward, Secretary of State, we tender our sympathy in his sufferings and our hope for his speedy recovery; and we assure him that the murderous attempt to remove him from his sphere of usefulness, has only strengthened him in the love and confidence of his countrymen."

The two Houses concurred after some refinements and issued the joint resolution on Friday, April 21, the day the Lincoln Funeral Train left the depot in Washington, D.C. The refinements made reference to the fact that the train would pass through "the principal cities on the line of the Central Railroad, and that a brief stop will be made in this city (Albany)."

They added further that a special committee of three from the Senate and five from the Assembly be appointed to "meet those having the remains of the deceased in charge, at the city of New York, and accompany them through the State; and that the Lieutenant-Governor be added to the committee as the chairman thereof."

Moreover, there was a provision requesting Governor Fenton to invite the Honorable Hamilton Fish, president of the State Society of Cincinnati, "and a committee of three of said society" to a meeting at the Capitol in Albany on Tuesday, April 25, at 10 a.m. "to concert measures to accompany the remains of our late President to Springfield, Illinois, and that His Excellency be hereby authorized and requested to make such suitable and proper arrangements as may be necessary for the occasion."

The "occasion" being that on that late Tuesday after dark the Lincoln Funeral Train would pull into an area near Albany and the remains of President Lincoln would be transported to the State Capitol itself.

It was further resolved that, "the people of the State should leave nothing undone to testify their love and solemn veneration for the heroic deeds and public services, reflecting luster on the country at large, of the late President, Abraham Lincoln, whose untimely death we are called to mourn."

Not surprisingly the resolution with its refinements passed both Houses by unanimous consent.

In connection with the resolution, a number of Assembly members spoke ,including the Honorable William Strong. Strong concluded:

"Four years ago this day (Friday, April 21, 1865), in the streets of Baltimore, the blood of our soldiers was shed while on their way to the protection of our national life.

"Today we meet in solemn sadness to mourn a greater calamity. Another martyr has been sacrificed upon the altar of our country. The blood of our murdered President stains the streets of our national capital, and cries aloud for justice. Eighteen hundred years ago our spiritual salvation was made possible, and already cemented all loyal hears upon one common purpose, and hereafter the spirit of Mercy will be attended with a sterner and more retributive Justice.

"We mourn, but not without hope."

Shortly afterwards, during that same dramatic year, Legislative Honors to the Memory of President Lincoln was printed in book form under the direction of J. B. Cushman, Clerk of the Assembly. The printers were Weed, Parsons and Company of Albany, New York.

Appendix 3

(Harper's Weekly)

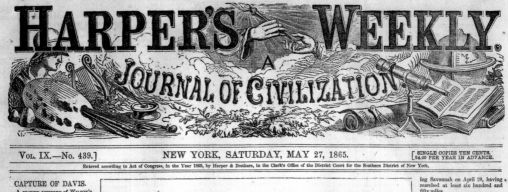

HARPER'S WEEKLY.

A JOURNAL OF CIVILIZATION

VOL. IX.—No. 439.]   NEW YORK, SATURDAY, MAY 27, 1865.   [SINGLE COPIES TEN CENTS. $4.00 PER YEAR IN ADVANCE.

Entered according to Act of Congress, in the Year 1865, by Harper & Brothers, in the Clerk's Office of the District Court for the Southern District of New York.

CAPTURE OF DAVIS.

A PICKED company of Wilson's command captured JEFFERSON DAVIS on the morning of May 10, at Irwinsville, Georgia. The company was commanded by Colonel PRITCHARD, of the Fourth Michigan. The following is General WILSON's dispatch announcing the capture:

MACON, GA., 9.30 A.M., May 13, 1865.

Hon. E. M. Stanton, Sec. of War:

Lieut.-Colonel HARDEN, commanding the First Wisconsin, has just arrived from Irwinsville. He struck the trail of DAVIS at Dublin, Laurens County, on the evening of the 7th, and followed him closely, night and day, through the pine wilderness to Alligator Creek and Green Swamp, via Cumberlandville to Irwinsville. At Cumberlandville Colonel HARDEN met Colonel PRITCHARD, with 150 picked men and horses of the Fourth Michigan. HARDEN followed the trail directly south, while PRITCHARD, having fresher horses, pushed down the Ocmulgee toward Hopewell, and thence by House Creek to Irwinsville, arriving there at midnight of the 9th. JEFF DAVIS had not arrived. From a citizen PRITCHARD learned that his party were encamped two miles out of the town. He made dispositions of his men, and surrounded the camp before day. HARDEN had camped at 9 P.M. within two miles, as he afterward learned, from DAVIS. The trail being too indistinct to follow, he pushed on at 3 A.M., and had gone but little more than one mile when his advance was fired upon by men of the Fourth Michigan. A fight ensued, both parties exhibiting the greatest determination. Fifteen minutes elapsed before

ing Savannah on April 28, having marched at least six hundred and fifty miles.

PAYNE THE ASSASSIN.

IN regard to LEWIS PAYNE, the assassin who entered Secretary SEWARD's sick room and inflicted upon him and his son wounds intended to prove fatal, little is yet publicly known. We publish his portrait on this page. Apparently he was a hired assassin dispatched from Canada. He is said to be an outlaw from Kentucky, and to have been concerned in the St. Albans raid and other schemes of murder and arson concocted in Canada. He was captured at Mrs. SURRATT's house in the disguise of a laboring man.

The course of the trial now going on at Washington will develop the biography of PAYNE—if indeed that be his real name. This trial has for its principal object not merely the conviction of PAYNE and ATZEROT, and the other tools of this base plot, but the disclosure of an extensive conspiracy. The agents in Richmond, and those in Canada, commissioned from Richmond—who they are, what they have attempted, and by what means—are the central objects about which this great trial revolves. It was for this reason

This is the cover of *Harper's Weekly* on May 27, 1865, which carried an account of the Lincoln funeral services in Springfield, Illinois.

In 1865, *Harper's Weekly* was the one of the most popular and widely read illustrated news magazines in the United States.

This page one story in the May 27, 1865 issue summed up the end of what had been thus far the most compelling and dramatic funeral train journey in history. It was simply headlined, "President Lincoln's Burial."

"It was a beautiful May day that President Lincoln was buried at Oak Ridge, Springfield. At noon the remains were brought from the State House in the same hearse which had carried Lyon and Thomas H. Benton to their graves.

"The hearse was surmounted by a beautiful crown of flowers. From the portico, as the procession advanced, a chorus of hundreds of voices sang the hymn—

'Children of the heavenly King,
Let us journey as we sing.'

"The Funeral Procession was under the immediate direction of General Hooker. The President's tomb is two miles from Springfield. A dirge was sung; and after the reading of Scripture, a prayer, and a hymn, the President's second Inaugural was read. A dirge succeeded, when Bishop Simpson delivered the funeral oration. It was in the highest degree eloquent and patriotic.

"We have," says a correspondent of the *Times*, "followed the remains from Washington, the scene of his assassination, to Springfield, his former home, and now to be his final resting place. He had been absent from this city ever since he left it in February, 1861, for the national capital, to be inaugurated as President of the United States.

"We have seen him lying in state in the Executive mansion, where the obsequies were attended by numerous mourners, some of them clothed with the highest public honors and responsibilities which our republican institutions can bestow, and by diplomatic representatives of foreign governments.

"We have followed the remains from Washington through Baltimore, Harrisburg, Philadelphia, New York, Albany, Buffalo, Cleveland, Columbus, Indianapolis, and Chicago to Springfield—a distance in circuit of 1,500 or 1,800 miles. On the route millions of people have appeared to manifest, by every means of which they are capable, their deep sense of the public loss, and their appreciation of the many virtues which adorned the life of Abraham Lincoln.

"All classes, without distinction of politics or creeds, spontaneously united in the posthumous honors.

"All hearts seemed to beat as one at the bereavement; and, now funeral processions are ended, our mournful duty of escorting the mortal remains of Abraham Lincoln hither is preformed. We have seen them deposited in the tomb.

"The bereaved friends, with subdued and grief-stricken hearts, have taken their adieu and turn their faces homeward, ever to remember the affecting and impressive scenes which they have witnessed.

"The injunction, so often repeated on the way, 'Bear him gently to his rest,' has been obeyed, and the great heart of the nation throbs heavily at the portals of the tomb."

Bibliography

Botts, John M. *The Great Rebellion: Its Secret History, Rise Progress, and Disastrous Failure.* (New York: Harper & Brothers, 1866)

Childebert, John W. *The Golden Tresure or a World of Knowledge.* (St.Louis, MO. James Mason, Publisher, 1890)

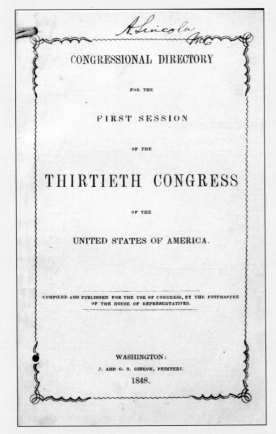

The Congressional Directory for the First Session of the 13th Congress of the United States. It signed at the top, "A. Lincoln MC." This publication in original blue wraps was published in Washington in 1848 by J. and G.S. Gideon. The volume was signed while Lincoln was serving as a Congressman from Illinois. At the time he was the only Whig representing the state of Illinois, and he served only one term from 1847 to 1849. During that term he served on the House Committee on Expenditures in the War Department. *Skinner, Inc.* estimated $14,000–$18,000.

Clark, Champ. *The Assassination: Death of a President.* (Alexandria, VA: Time-Life Books, 1987)

Coffin, Charles C. *Abraham Lincoln.* (New York: Harper & Brothers, 1893)

Coggshall, William T. *Lincoln Memorial: The Journeys of Abraham Lincoln: From Springfield to Washington, 1861, as President Elect; and from Washington to Springfield, 1865, as President Martyred.* (Columbus: Ohio State Journal, 1865)

Cullen, Jim. *The Civil War in Popular Culture: A Reusable Past.* (Washington, D.C.: Smithsonian Institution Press, 1995)

Dana, Charles A. *Recollections of the Civil War: With the Leaders in Washington and in the Field in the Sixties.* (New York: D. Appleton, 1889)

DeWitt, David Miller. *The Assassination of Abraham Lincoln and Its Expiation.* (New York: Macmillan, 1909)

Donald, David H. *Lincoln.* (New York: Simon & Schuster, 1995)

Durant, John and Alice. *Pictorial History of American Presidents.* (New York, N.Y.:A.S. Barnes and Company, 1958)

Eisenchiml, Otto. *In the Shadow of Lincoln's Death.* (New York: Wilfred Funk, 1940)

Furman, Bess. *White House Profile.* (Indianapolis: The Bobbs-Merrill Company, Inc., 1951)

Greene, Laurence. *America Goes to Press: Headlines of the Past.* (Indianapolis: Bobbs-Merrill Company, 1936)

Harris, T.M. *Assassination of Lincoln: A History of the Great Conspiracy, American Citizens Company.* (New York)

Jenson, Oliver. *The American Heritage History of Railroads in America.* (New York: American Heritage Publishing Co. Inc., 1975)

Judson, Edward Z. *The Parricides; or, the Doom of the Assassins, the Authors of the Nation's Loss, by Ned Buntline.* (New York: Hilton & Co., 1865)

Kane, Joseph N. *Facts About the Presidents.* (New York, N.Y.: The H.W. Wilson Company, 1959)

Kunhardt, Dorothy Meserve, and Philip B. Kunhardt Jr. *Twenty Days.* (New York: Harper & Row,1960)

Lamon, Dorothy, editor. *Recollections of Abraham Lincoln, 1847-1865.* (Chicago: A. C. McClurg and Co., 1895)

Leech, Margeret. *Reveille in Washington, 1860-1865.* (New York: Harper & Brothers,1941)

Lerch, Kathryn W., editor. *Words of War: The Park Tudor Legacy Initiative.* (Guild Press-Emmis Publishing, Zionsville, IN., 2001)

Lowenfels, Walter, editor. *Walt Whitman's Civil War.* (New York: Knopf, 1960)

McPherson, James M. *Battle Cry of Freedom: The Civil War Era.* (New York: Oxford University Press, 1988)

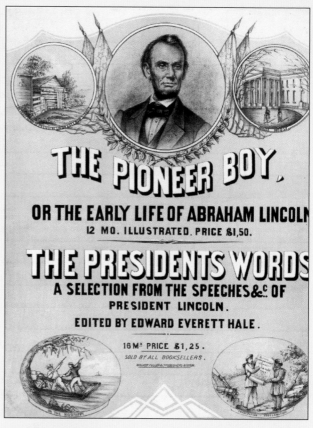

The Pioneer Boy, Or The Early Life of Abraham Lincoln, and *The Presidents Words—A Selection From the Speeches of President Lincoln* edited by Edward Everett Hale. This poster promotes two publications about Lincoln, available by subscription. There were also numerous books issued in 1865 and in the years immediately following President Lincoln's death about his life and times. *Skinner, Inc.*

Morris, B.F. *Memorial Record of the Nation's Tribute to Abraham Lincoln.* (Washington, D.C.: W.H. & O.H. Morrison, 1865)

Shea, John Gilmary. *The Lincoln Memorial: A Record of the Life, Assassination, and Obsequies of the Martyred President.* (New York: Bruce & Huntington, 1865)

Murphy, Jim. *The Boys' War-Confederate and Union Soldiers Talk About the Civil War.* (New York: Scholastic Inc. 1990)

Neely, Mark Jr. *The Abraham Lincoln Encyclopedia.* (New York: McGraw-Hill, 1982)

Newman, Ralph G. *In This Sad World: A Timetable for the Lincoln Train.* (Springfield, IL: Civil War Centennial Commission, 1965)

Oates, Stephen. *With Malice Toward None: The Life of Abraham Lincoln.* (New York: Harper & Row, 1977)

Ostendorf, Lloyd. *Lincoln's Photographs: A Complete Album.* (Dayton, OH: Rockywood Press, 1998)

Petersen, Merrill D. *Lincoln in American Memory.* (New York: Oxford University Press, 1994)

Peterson, T. B. *Illustrated Life, Services, Martyrdom, and Funeral of Abraham Lincoln.* (Philadelphia: T. B. Peterson & Brothers, 1865)

Peterson, T.B. *The Trial of the Alleged Assassins and Conspirators at Washington*

Abrahán Lincoln
Presidente de los Estados Unidos
de America, quien llevó a cabo
la emancipación de la esclavitud
1809-1865.   F.M.

A Mexican postcard pays tribute to President Abraham Lincoln, and also noted the date of his birth and death.

City, D.C. (Philadelphia: T. B. Peterson & Brothers, 1865)

Pinkerton, Allan. *History and Evidence of the Passage of Abraham Lincoln form Harrisburg, PA. to Washington, D.C.* (Chicago: Republican Press, 1868)

Pitman, Benn. *The Assassination of President Lincoln and the Trial of the Conspirators.* (Cincinnati, OH: Moore, Wilstach & Baldwin, 1865)

Plowden, David. *Lincoln and His America.* (New York: Viking Press, 1970)

Power, John Carroll. *Abraham Lincoln: His Life, Public Services, Death and Great Funeral Cortege.* (Chicago and Springfield, IL.: H.W. Rokker, 1889)

Reed, Robert M. *Colonial Law in America.* (Schiffer Publishing, Atglen, PA, 2011)

Reed, Robert M. *The United States Presidents Illustrated.* (Schiffer Publishing, Atglen, PA. 2009)

Reilly, Bernard F. Jr. *American Political Prints 1766-1876: A Catalog of the Collections in the Library of Congress.* (Boston: G.K. Hall & Co., 1991)

Sermons Preached in Boston on the Death of Abraham Lincoln, Together with the Funeral Services in the East Room of the Executive Mansion at Washington. (Boston: J. E. Tilton & Co., 1865)

Searcher, Victor. *The Farewell to Lincoln.* (New York: Abingdon Press, 1965)

Shaw, Archer H. *The Lincoln Encyclopedia.* (New York: Macmillan, 1950)

Shea, John Gilmary, editor. *The Lincoln Memorial: A Record of the Life, Assassination and Obsequies of the Martyred President.* (New York: Bruce & Huntington, 1865)

Smoot, Richard. *The Unwritten History of the Assassination of Abraham Lincoln.* (Clinton, MA.:W.J. Coulter, 1908)

Snyder, Louis and Richard Morris, editors. *A Treasury Of Great Reporting.* (New York: Simon and Schuster, 1949)

Spencer, William V. *Lincolniana: In Memoriam.* (Boston: William V. Spencer, 1865.)

Steers, Edward Jr. *Blood on the Moon: The Assassination of Abraham Lincoln.* (Lexington: University of Kentucky Press, 2001)

The Terrible Tragedy at Washington: Assassination of President Lincoln. (Philadelphia: Barclay & Co., 1865)

Thomas, Benjamin P. *Abraham Lincoln.* (New York: Knopf, 1952)

Townsend, George Alfred. *The Life, Crime and Capture of John Wilkes Booth.* (New York: Dick and Fitzgerald, 1865)

Trostel, Scott D. *The Lincoln Funeral.* (Fletcher, OH: Cam-Tech Publishing, 2002)

U.S. War Department. *The War of the Rebellion: A Compilation of the Official Records of the Union and Confederate Armies, 128 vols.* (Washington, D.C.: Government Printing Office, 1890-1901)

Valentine, David T. *Obsequies of Abraham Lincoln, in the City of New York.* (New York: Edmund Jones & Co., 1866)

Weosolowski, Wayne and Mary Cay. *The Lincoln Train is Coming.* (Leslie: Illinois Benedictine College, 1995)

Wilson, Francis. *John Wilkes Booth: Fact and Fiction of Lincoln's Assassination.* (Boston: Houghton Mifflin, 1929)

Periodicals and Newspapers

Associated Press
Boston Daily Advertiser
Buffalo (NY)Daily Express
Chicago Times
Chicago Tribune

Illinois Journal
Indiana (Ips.) Journal
National Daily Intelligencer
Philadelphia Inquirer
Philadelphia Public Ledger
New Castle (IN) Courier
New York Herald
New York Times
New-York Tribune
Richmond (VA) Whig
Sing Sing (NY) Republican
Springfield (IL)Register
Washington Evening Star

Abraham Lincoln
Born in Hardin County Ky. February 12 1809
President of the United States
4 years 1 month, 11 days
Died in Washington April 15 1865

Memorial postcard showing the time President Abraham Lincoln served in the White House, and the date of his death in Washington, D.C.

Introduction

"not just by the thousands...": *Philadelphia Enquirer*, April 24, 1865; also quoted in *Lincoln Memorial: The Journeys of Abraham Lincoln: From Springfield to Washington* and *From Washington to Springfield* by William T. Coggshall, 1865.

Chapter One
Journey Begins

"One million dollars wanted...": An account from the *Selma (Alabama) Dispatch*, 1864 as noted in *America Goes to Press: Headlines of the Past* by Laurence Greene. 1936.

"A man named Clements...": Address by Schuyler Colfax, Chicago, April 30, 1865 quoting *Philadelphia North American*, March 8, 1865; also reported in America Goes to Press by Laurence Greene, 1936.

"On the morning of April 14...": Quote from the *National Daily Intelligencer* as noted in *America Goes to Press* by Lawrence Greene, 1936.

"Lieutenant General Grant...": *Washington Evening Star*, April 14, 1865; also noted in *America Goes to Press* by Laurence Greene, 1936.

"Like a clap of thunder...": *New-York Tribune*, April 15, 1865; also noted in *A Treasury of Great Reporting* edited by Louis Snyder and Richard Morris, 1949.

"The sad story...": *Philadelphia Public Ledger*, April, 1865; also noted in *America Goes to Press* by Laurence Greene, 1936.

"The undersigned is directed...": *Abraham Lincoln: His Life, Public Services, Death and Great Funeral Cortege* by John C. Power, 1889.

"The procession will move...": *Abraham Lincoln: His Life, Public Services, Death and Great Funeral Cortege* by John C. Power, 1889.

"As various delegations came...": *Illustrated Life: Services, Martyrdom, And Funeral of Abraham Lincoln* by T.B. Peterson, 1865.

"Weak, worn and nervous...": *The Life, Crime and Capture of John Wilkes Booth* by George Alfred Townsend, 1865.

"Death has fastened...": *The Life, Crime and Capture of John Wilkes Booth* by George Alfred Townsend, 1865.

"Retained their sweet, placid...": *Lincoln Memorial: The Journeys of Abraham Lincoln...From Washington to Springfield* by William T. Coggshall, 1865.

"Not less than 5,000 officers...": *The Life, Crime and Capture of John Wilkes Booth* by George Alfred Townsend, 1865.

"...insignias of sorrow profusely displayed...": *Abraham Lincoln: His Life, Public Services, Death and Great Funeral Cortege* by John C. Power, 1889.

"....with proper mourning drapery...": *Lincoln, His Life, Public Services, Death and Great Funeral Cortege* by John C. Power, 1889.

"...by one simultaneous movement...": *Lincoln, His Life, Public Services, Death and Great Funeral Cortege* by John C. Power, 1889.

"...men labored upon the monument...": *Lincoln, His Life, Public Services, Death and Great Funeral Cortege* by John C. Power, 1889.

"....because it is the desire of military authorities...": An account from the *Richmond (Virginia) Whig* as noted in *America Goes To Press* by Laurence Greene, 1936.

"It is hoped that politicians will be sufficiently restrained...": An account from the *Philadelphia Public Ledger* as noted in *America Goes To Press* by Laurence Greene, 1936.

"It has been finally concluded...": Official Records, War of the Rebellion, Washington, D.C. 1890-1901.

"Lincoln's complexion had always been dark...": *The Life, Crime And Capture of John Wilkes Booth* by George Alfred Townsend, 1865.

"...all persons disobeying the orders..." *Lincoln, His Life, Public Services, Death and Great Funeral Cortege* by John C. Power, 1889.

"...and a greater number if the road can command them..." : *Lincoln, His Life, Public Services, Death and Great Funeral Cortege* by John C. Power., 1889.

"...over the route...": *Lincoln, His Life, Public Services, Death and Great Funeral Cortege* by John C. Power, 1889.

"A portion of the soldiers...": *Lincoln, His Life, Public Services, Death and Great Funeral Cortege* by John C. Power, 1889.

Chapter Two
Northward

"Here the people...": Official Rules and Regulations, War Department's Adjutant General's Office, April 20, 1865—*U.S. War Department Official Records*, War of the Rebellion, Washington, D.C. 1890-1901.

"As the train moved on to Camden Station...": *Services, Martyrdom, and Funeral of Abraham Lincoln* by T.B. Peterson, 1865.

"Work was suspended...": *Lincoln Memorial: The Journeys of Abraham Lincoln—From Washington to Springfield* by William T. Coggshall, 1865.

"...its mournful march back to Camden Station...": *Lincoln Memorial: The Journeys of Abraham Lincoln—From Washington to Springfield* by William T. Coggshall,1865.

"....dressed in black were kindly permitted...": *Lincoln Memorial: The Journeys of Abraham Lincoln—From Washington to Springfield* by William T. Coggshall, 1865.

"Silently they preformed...": *Lincoln Memorial: The Journeys of Abraham Lincoln—From Washington to Springfield* by William T. Coggshall, 1865.

"On the 21st I was in the city...": *Words of War: The Park Tudor Legacy Initiative* edited by Kathryn Lerch; and The U.S National Archives.

"The remains were escorted...": *Abraham Lincoln: His Life , Public Services, Death and Great Funeral Cortege* by John C. Power, 1889.

"At the outskirts of town...": *Abraham Lincoln: His Life, Public Services, Death and Great Funeral Cortege* by John C. Power, 1889.

"Here the people were counted...": *Philadelphia Enquirer*, April 24, 1865; also quoted in the *Lincoln Memorial: The Journeys of Abraham Lincoln—From Washington to Springfield* by William T. Coggshall, 1865.

"It move through the wide and bountiful streets...": *Abraham Lincoln: His Life, Public Services, Death and Great Funeral Cortege* by John C. Power, 1889.

"The interior of the hall...": *Abraham Lincoln: His Life, Public Services, Death and Great Funeral Cortege* by John C. Power, 1889.

"As the draped cars passed...": *Illustrated Life, Services, Martyrdom, and Funeral of Abraham Lincoln* by T. B. Peterson, 1865.

"Every hill top on the line...": *Lincoln Memorial: The Journeys of Abraham Lincoln—From Washington to Springfield* by William T. Coggshall, 1865.

"A detachment of the reserved veterans...": *Lincoln Memorial: The Journeys of Abraham Lincoln—From Washington to Springfield* by William T. Coggshall, 1865.

"Its location...": *Abraham Lincoln: His Life, Public Services, Death and Great Funeral Cortege* by John C. Power, 1889.

"All of Newark...": *Lincoln Memorial: The Journeys of Abraham Lincoln—From Washington to Springfield* by William T. Coggshall, 1865.

"There was a great procession here...": Original Civil War letter in the possession of the Early American Store.

"For more than a mile...": *Abraham Lincoln: His Life, Public Services, Death and Great Funeral Cortege* by John C. Power, 1889.

"At so many points...": *Illustrated Life, Services, Martyrdom, and Funeral of Abraham Lincoln* by T.B. Peterson, 1865.

"As the remains were conveyed...": *Abraham Lincoln: His Life, Public Services, Death and Great Funeral Cortege* by John C. Powers, 1889.

———※———

Chapter Three
Westward

"...was in keeping...": *Abraham Lincoln His Life, Public Services, Death, and Great Funeral Cortege* by John C. Power, 1889.

"As far as the eye could see...": *Lincoln Memorial: The Journeys of Abraham Lincoln—From Washington to Springfield* by William T. Coggshall, 1865.

"The coffin rested...": *Illustrated Life, Services, Martyrdom and Funeral* of Abraham Lincoln by T.B. Peterson, 1865.

"...not understand such vast numbers...": *Abraham Lincoln His Life, Public Services, Death and Great Funeral Cortege* by John C. Power, 1889.

"They came in glittering...": *Lincoln Memorial: The Journeys of Abraham Lincoln—From Washington to Springfield* by William T. Coggshall, 1865.

"...standing in a dense...": *Illustrated Life, Services, Martyrdom, and Funeral of Abraham Lincoln* by T. B. Peterson, 1865.

"Mourning emblems...": *Abraham Lincoln: His Life, Public Services, Death and Great Funeral Cortege* by John C. Power, 1889.

"The more I think of the subject...": *Lincoln Memorial: The Journeys of Abraham Lincoln—From Washington to Springfield* by William T. Coggshall,1865.

"All things being in readiness...": *Abraham Lincoln: His Life, Public Services, Death and Great Funeral Cortege* by John C. Power, 1889.

"It happened...": *Lincoln Memorial: The Journeys of Abraham Lincoln—From Washington to Springfield* by William T. Coggshall, 1865.

"...a bounteous supper...": *Abraham Lincoln: His Life, Public Services, Death and Great Funeral Cortege* by John C. Power, 1889.

"After a stay...": *Lincoln Memorial: The Journeys of Abraham Lincoln—From Washington to Springfield* by William T. Coggshall, 1865.

"A torchlight procession...": *Abraham Lincoln: His Life, Public Services, Death and Great Funeral Cortege* by John C. Power, 1889.

"Thousands of people...": *Abraham Lincoln: His Life, Public Services, Death and Great Funeral Cortege* by John C., Power, 1889.

"Arrived to find the depot...": *Lincoln Memorial: The Journeys of Abraham Lincoln—From Washington to Springfield* by William T. Coggshall, 1865.

"The streets were thronged...": *Lincoln Memorial: The Journeys of Abraham Lincoln—From Washington to Springfield* by William T. Coggshall, 1865.

"The crowd...": *Abraham Lincoln: His Life, Public Services, Death and Great Funeral Cortege* by John C. Power, 1889.

"Solemn dirges...": *Illustrated Life, Services, Martyrdom, and Funeral of Abraham Lincoln* by T. B. Peterson, 1865.

"From the time...": *Abraham Lincoln: His Life, Public Services, Death and Great Funeral Cortege* by John C. Power, 1889.

"Never before...": *Abraham Lincoln, His Life, Public Services, Death, and Great Funeral Cortege* by John C. Power, 1889.

"The women were much affected...": *Abraham Lincoln: His Life, Public Services, Death and Great Funeral Cortege* by John C. Power, 1889.

"The train passed through an arch...": *Lincoln Memorial: The Journeys of Abraham Lincoln—From Washington to Springfield* by William T. Coggshall, 1865.

"When the train arrived at St. Johnsville...": *Abraham Lincoln: His Life, Public Services, Death and Great Funeral Cortege* by John C. Power, 1889.

"It was now quite dark...": *Abraham Lincoln: His Life, Public Services, Death and Great Funeral Cortege* by John C. Powers, 1889.

"Those on board the train...": *Abraham Lincoln: His Life, Public Services, Death and Great Funeral Cortege* by John C. Powers, 1889.

"...as the train swept by Whitesboro...": *Lincoln Memorial-The Journeys of Abraham*

Lincoln—From Washington to Springfield by William T. Coggshall, 1865.

"...the coffin was overshadowed...": *Abraham Lincoln His Life, Public Services, Death and Great Funeral Cortege* by John C. Power, 1889.

"The principle feature of the scene...": *Lincoln Memorial: The Journeys of Abraham Lincoln—From Washington to Springfield* by William T. Coggshall, 1889.

"The citizens of Erie...": *Abraham Lincoln: His Life, Public Services, Death and Great Funeral Cortege* by John C. Power, 1889.

"Between Buffalo and Cleveland...": *Lincoln Memorial: The Journeys of Abraham Lincoln—From Washington to Springfield* by William T. Coggshall, 1865.

❦

Chapter Four
Heartland

"An immense multitude...": *Abraham Lincoln: His Life, Public Services, Death and Great Funeral Cortege* by John C. Power, 1889.

"Every train that arrived...": *Lincoln Memorial: The Journeys of Abraham Lincoln—From Washington to Springfield* by William T. Coggshall, 1865.

"...the symbols of mourning...": *Lincoln Memorial: The Journeys of Abraham Lincoln—From Washington to Springfield* by William T. Coggshall, 1865.

"Along the line designated..." *Lincoln Memorial: The Journeys of Abraham Lincoln—From Washington to Springfield* by William T. Coggshall, 1865.

"This temple...": *Abraham Lincoln: His Life, Death and Great Funeral Cortege* by John C. Power, 1889.

"And many a bronzed...": *Lincoln Memorial: The Journeys of Abraham Lincoln—From Washington to Springfield* by William T. Coggshall, 1865.

"Up to the last...": *Lincoln Memorial: The Journeys of Abraham Lincoln—From Washington to Springfield* by William T. Coggshall, 1865.

"Among the towns...": *Abraham Lincoln: His Life, Public Services, Death and Great Funeral Cortege* by John C. Power, 1889.

Order of Procession—Lincoln Memorial: *The Journeys of Abraham Lincoln—From Washington to Springfield* by William T. Coggshall, 1865; and the *U.S. War Department Official Records*, War of the Rebellion, Washington, D.C.—1890-1901.

"The pillars...": *Abraham Lincoln: His Life, Public Services, Death and Great Funeral Cortege* by John C. Power, 1889.

"The walls were adorned...": *Abraham Lincoln: His Life, Public Services, Death and Great Funeral Cortege* by John C. Power, 1889.

"There was not...": *Lincoln Memorial: The Journeys of Abraham Lincoln—From Washington to Springfield* by William T. Coggshall, 1865.

"...giving personal attention...": *Lincoln Memorial: The Journeys of Abraham Lincoln—From Washington to Springfield* by William T. Coggshall, 1865.

"A patriotic religious song...": *Lincoln Memorial: The Journeys of Abraham Lincoln—From Washington to Springfield* by William T. Coggshall, 1865.

"...were passed...": *Abraham Lincoln: His Life, Death and Great Funeral Cortege* by John C. Power, 1889.

"The depot..." *Abraham Lincoln: His Life, Death and Great Funeral Cortege* by John C. Power, 1889.

"At the time appointed...": *Abraham Lincoln: His Life, Death and Great Funeral Cortege* by John C. Power, 1889.

"Not only were...": *Lincoln Memorial: The Journeys of Abraham Lincoln—From Washington to Springfield* by William T. Coggshall, 1865.

"The depot at Centerville...": *Abraham Lincoln: His Life, Public Services, and Great Funeral Cortege* by John C. Power, 1889.

"The people were anxious...": *Abraham Lincoln: His Life, Public Services, and Great Funeral Cortege* by John C. Power, 1889.

"Eventually the darkness...": *Illustrated Life, Services, Martyrdom, and Funeral of Abraham Lincoln* by T. B. Peterson, 1865.

"It was the unanimous verdict...": *Abraham Lincoln: His Life, Public Services, and Great Funeral Cortege* by John C. Power, 1889.

"There was a solemn...": *Illustrated Life, Services, Martyrdom, and Funeral of Abraham Lincoln* by T. B. Peterson, 1865.

"Their looks...": *Lincoln Memorial: The Journeys of Abraham Lincoln—From Washington to Springfield* by William T. Coggshall, 1865.

"And although...": *Abraham Lincoln: His Life, Public Services, and Great Funeral Cortege* by John C. Power, 1889.

"Mourning emblems...": *Abraham Lincoln: His Life, Public Service, and Great Funeral Cortege* by John C. Power, 1889.

"The avenues leading to the depot...": *Abraham Lincoln: His Life, Death and Great Funeral Cortege* by John C. Powers, 1889.

"All the streets...": *Lincoln Memorial: The Journeys of Abraham Lincoln—From Washington to Springfield* by William T. Coggshall, 1865.

"The colored Masons...": *Abraham Lincoln: His Life, Death and Great Funeral Cortege* by John C. Power, 1889.

"The depots were draped...": *Lincoln Memorial: The Journeys of Abraham Lincoln—From Washington to Springfield* by William T. Coggshall, 1865.

"It was known...": *Abraham Lincoln: His Life, Death and Great Funeral Cortege* by John C. Power, 1889.

"And the people in many ways...": *Abraham Lincoln: His Life, Death and Great Funeral Cortege* by John C. Power, 1889.

"After all had partaken...": *Lincoln Memorial: The Journeys of Abraham Lincoln—From Washington to Springfield* by William T. Coggshall, 1865.

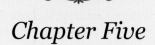

Chapter Five
Homeland

"As the train neared Chicago...": *Lincoln Memorial: The Journeys of Abraham Lincoln—From Washington to Springfield* by William T. Coggshall, 1865.

"It was sufficiently elevated...": *Abraham Lincoln: His Life, Death and Great Funeral Cortege* by John C. Power, 1889.

"Every window...": *Lincoln Memorial: The Journeys of Abraham Lincoln—From Washington to Springfield* by William T. Coggshall, 1865.

"Next were the...": *Lincoln Memorial: The Journeys of Abraham Lincoln—From Washington to Springfield* by William T. Coggshall, 1865.

"It was a wilderness of banners...": *Abraham Lincoln: His Life, Death and Great Funeral Cortege* by John C. Power, 1889.

"Tens of thousands...": *Abraham Lincoln: His Life, His Death and Great Funeral Cortege* by John C. Power, 1889.

"The arrangements...": *Lincoln Memorial: The Journeys of Abraham Lincoln—From Washington to Springfield* by William T. Coggshall, 1865.

"And yet it was...": *Illustrated Life, Services, Martyrdom, and Funeral of Abraham Lincoln* by T. B. Peterson, 1865.

"The skill and judgment...": *Abraham Lincoln: His Life, Public Services, and Great Funeral Cortege* by John C. Power, 1889.

"I have seen three..." quote from eyewitness as noted in *Abraham Lincoln: His Life, Public Services, and Great Funeral Cortege* by John C. Power, 1889.

"...probably not more...": *Lincoln Memorial: The Journeys of Abraham Lincoln—From Washington to Springfield* by William T. Coggshall, 1865.

"The remains had tarried...": *Abraham Lincoln: His Life, Public Services, and Great Funeral Cortege* by John C. Power 1889.

"The glare of light...": *Abraham Lincoln: His Life, Public Services, and Great Funeral Cortege* by John C. Power, 1889.

"The American flag...": *Lincoln Memorial: The Journeys of Abraham Lincoln—From Washington to Springfield* by William T. Coggshall, 1865.

"There would, no doubt...": *Abraham Lincoln: His Life, Public Services, and Great Funeral Cortege* by John C. Power, 1889.

"A profuse display...": *Lincoln Memorial: The Journeys of Abraham Lincoln—From Washington to Springfield* by William T. Coggshall, 1865.

"Many people...": *Lincoln Memorial : The Journeys of Abraham Lincoln—from Washington to Springfield* by William T. Coggshall, 1865.

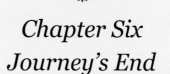

Chapter Six
Journey's End

"The great anxiety...": *Abraham Lincoln: His Life, Death and Great Funeral Cortege* by John C. Power, 1889.

"As for sleeping...": *Abraham Lincoln, His Life, Death and Great Funeral Cortege* by John C. Power, 1889.

"The city is so crowded...": *Lincoln Memorial: The Journeys of Abraham Lincoln—From Washington to Springfield* by William T. Coggshall, 1865.

"The ten minutes...": *Abraham Lincoln: His Life, Death and Great Funeral Cortege* by John C. Power, 1889.

"Strangers who were...": *Abraham Lincoln: His Life, Death and Great Funeral Cortege* by John C. Power, 1889.

"No human voices...": *Abraham Lincoln: His Life, Death and Great Funeral Cortege* by John C. Power, 1889.

"Never before...": *Illustrated Life, Services, Martyrdom, and Funeral of Abraham Lincoln* by T.B. Peterson, 1865.

"On arriving...": *Abraham Lincoln: His Life, Death and Great Funeral Cortege* by John C. Power, 1889.

"The landscape...": *Illustrated Life, Services, Martyrdom, and Funeral of Abraham Lincoln* by T.B. Peterson, 1865.

"When the vast multitude...": *Abraham Lincoln: His Life, Death, and Great Funeral Cortege* by John C. Power, 1889.

Index

A quotation of President Abraham Lincoln featured on early 1900s postcard.

Hough, Col. R.M.104, 108
Houghtonville, NJ 48
Howe, A. P.29
Hudson, NY 61, 69
Hudson River Railway 57, 58, 67
Hunter, Gen. David 29
Hunter, William 18, 67, 83
Hyde Park, NY 69
Hyde Park Township 102

I

Indianapolis, IN 11, 14, 25, 81, 84, 89-90,
    92-93, 95-100, 132, 138
Iberia, OH 87
Ilion, NY 65, 69
Intersection, PA 45
Irving, NY 70
Irvington, NY 59, 69

J

Jersey City, NJ 48
Jessups, MD 35
Joliet, IL 110, 111, 113, 124, 132
Jordon, NY 70
Jordan, OH 87

K

Kankokee, IN 97, 100
Kenny, IL 113
Kensington, IN 44, 45, 100
Kingsville, OH 73
Kirkville, NY 66, 70
Knightstown, IN 8-10, 42, 99, 100, 132

L

LaCroix, IN 97, 100
LaCrosse, IN 97, 100
Lafayette, IN 97, 100, 132
Lafayette Junction, IN 100
LaGrange, OH 79, 87
Lake Calumet 102
Lake Ford, IL 113
Lake View, NY 70
Lamson Brothers Co. 72

Lancaster, NY 66, 70
Lancaster, PA 37, 38, 45
Landisville, PA 37, 45
Lane, OH 87
Laurel, MD 35
Leaman Place, PA 45
Lebanon, IN 97, 100
Lemont, IL 110, 113
Leonardsburg, OH 87
Lewis Center, OH 79, 87
Lewisville, IN 92, 99, 100
Lexington, IL 112, 113
Light Guard Band 76, 109
Lincoln, IL 113
Lincoln, Mary Todd 15, 20, 28, 127
Lincoln, Robert 20, 28, 126
Lincoln, William "Willie" 27
Linden, NJ 48
Lochtel, PA 45
Lockport, IL 110, 113
Lowry, Thomas 130
Little Falls, NY 64, 69
Lutherville, MD 36

M

Madison, OH 73, 87
Manhattanville, NY 51, 69
Manlius, NY 70
Mantua, PA 45
Marble Cliff, OH 87
Mather, Col. Thomas 36, 37
McCallum, D.C 29.
McClean, IL 113
McClellan, Gen. George 10, 92
Merchants' Exchange 35
Meridian, NY 70
Merion, PA 45
Metuchen, NY 45
Michigan City, IN 78, 97-100
Milford Center, OH 87
Mill Creek, PA 71
Millstone Junction, NJ 48
Mississippi & Missouri Railroad 129
Mohawk River 63
Moneton, MD 36
Monmouth Junction, NJ 48
Morgan's Corner, PA 45

First day cover of the 100th Anniversary of the President Lincoln Funeral Train in Indianapolis, on April 30, 1965.

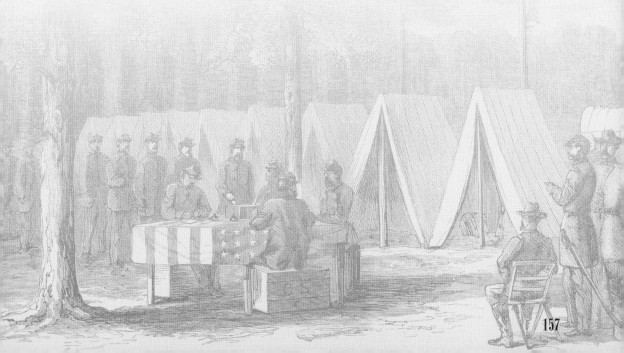

Yours truly
A. Lincoln

Robert M. Reed has been writing about antiques, collectibles and American history for the past quarter of a century. He has written 18 books. His latest book, *Colonial Law in America*, was nominated for a national book award.

For more than 30 years, Robert has also been a resident of one of the many communities that was a station and a stop for the historic Lincoln Funeral Train of 1865.